I've known Thi'sl for [...] impact people all around the [...] handful of people in our day like him, who came out the fire and have turned back around to run back into it to pull people out. His voice is special, unique and challenging. He reminds us of what we should all be doing with our lives—living for something greater than ourselves.

— Lecrae
Grammy Award Winning Artist, Actor,
Co-Owner of Reach Records

The life story of Thi'sl is nothing less than astounding. His journey has left a profound impact on me and I have retold it to numerous people. Read these words and let this story challenge yours.

— Judah Smith
Author, Pastor of The City Church
(Seattle, Washington)

Listening to Thi'sl's music and hearing him speak shows how people can change for the better. He has seen the worst and now he is seeing the best in people! Thi'sl's story has inspired and will continue to inspire people all across the world!

— Bubba Watson
Two-time PGA Masters Champion

AGAINST ALL ODDS

Travis Thi'sl Tyler

Foreword by FLAME

Against All Odds

Copyright © 2016 by Travis Thi'sl Tyler

Unless otherwise noted Scripture quotations are from The Holy Bible, English Standard Version® (ESV®), copyright © 2001 by Crossway, a publishing ministry of Good News Publishers. Used by permission. All rights reserved.

Published by: Travis Thi'sl Tyler / Full Ride Music Group, LLC.

Cover Design by: Larissa Leaper

Interior Design by: Mona Scheier

Editing by: Michelle Murray

Author Photo: Ed Rhone

Library of Congress Registration # TXu 1-965-107

ISBN: 978-0-9970059-0-5

10 9 8 7 6 5 4 3 2 1

Autobiography / Personal Growth / Christian

First Edition

Printed in The United States of America

TABLE OF CONTENTS

DEDICATION

Writing this book has made me realize how unique my life has been and how many people have sacrificed for me to get here. I want to dedicate this book to every teacher who had me as a student and believed in me even when I was in their class acting a fool, especially my learning enrichment teacher, Ms. Crockett. She was one of the first people who believed in my ability to write and took the time to shape it.

I also want to dedicate this to my grandfather who worked hard to give his family a better life.

To my wife, my A-1, my best friend—we went through the struggle together and she is still standing beside me today.

To my children, who I pray will one day understand the sacrifices that were made so they would not see a life like the one I lived and talk about in this book.

FOREWORD

I remember as a young kid listening to stories from my grandmother about her Christian experience. I would sit on her orange and khaki couch as she shared with me things God had done in her life. The tales were always dramatic and full of action. Her vocal tones would exhibit perfect pitch as she took me on her journey through the inner city streets of St. Louis. As she reached the climax of the story, I would be on the edge of my seat waiting to hear how the story would end. Jesus was always at the center of her stories with a triumphant entry and rescue.

At 16 years old, I became a Christian myself. One of the things the Lord used to draw me to Himself was the testimony of my grandmother. God was always the hero and was depicted in her experiences as a good God who seeks to save the lost. Now I had come to know Him as my Savior. One of the things I learned as a new Christian was that God wasn't done with His rescue mission of sinners. He was still creating stories to show His goodness and salvation.

Not too long after I surrendered to God, I met a guy known as "Unk," who was well-known, feared, and respected on the west side of St. Louis. Little did I know, God was about to demonstrate His power to change a hard heart right before my eyes. With a front row seat, I watched God take "Unk" and convict him of his sin and give him an unquenchable desire to live righteously and to make an impact in the same streets he was saved from. After changing his name to Thi'sl (This House I Shall Live), he began to compose music that chronicled his life's journey and God's redemption.

3

I had the privilege of witnessing God transfer Thi'sl from darkness to light, or to put it another way, from goon to Godly. There are unique struggles and barriers that need particular attention for the urban dweller. Travis Thi'sl Tyler has crafted a one of a kind book that invites us along to witness his story of redemption. If ever there was a time for such relevant material, it is now.

Marcus T. Williams Grey, a.k.a. FLAME

ACKNOWLEDGMENTS

I think it would be appropriate to start by saying that I am just happy to be alive right now, and after you read this story you may say the same. There are a lot of people who did not make it through this story, a lot of people whose lives and deaths shaped my life. I want to thank God for the friends I met during one of the worst times in my life: James, J.R., Marcus T. Williams Grey (a.k.a. FLAME), and Stephan. God sent you all at a point when I needed to learn to trust again, and you all helped me get there.

I have to give a big thanks to my beautiful, strong, loving, mother. Despite her struggles when I was growing up, the main thing I remember about her is the sacrifice and love that she had for my brother and I. I got my grind and hustle from Momma. It didn't matter what she did or how crazy life was, she got up and went to work. You are a queen, Momma, and I can never repay you for what you have done for me. Thank you for always being in my corner and fighting for me.

My granny, oh Lord, how I love that woman. It didn't matter what I was doing in the street, she still loved me like I was her innocent baby boy. Her presence reminded me that God was real. Her home was a refuge for me, and her words could cut me and heal me like no one else's that I knew. God gave me that woman to remind me of beauty in a cold world. I miss her so much every day. I spent the last five years of her life taking care of her and serving her, like she had done for me for so many for years, and I would do it all over again without a thought. I love you, Granny!

My Grandfather, Samuel D. Billingsley, Sr...thank you, Granddaddy, for being a pillar to our family. Thank you for taking me in and putting up with all of my lying and foolishness over the years. You are the reason I've always wanted to work for myself. You are the reason I love cars. I've always looked up to you and I've always wanted to make you proud. Love you, Granddaddy! Thank you for getting us off of that plantation!

Pastor George White, Jr., the first man who ever stood up for me and didn't have a thing to gain from it—thank you for being by my side in such a crazy time. I was afraid and lost, but your presence in that situation made it easier to deal with. Thank you!

I could go on and on about people who have loved me through this crazy life of mine and people who have sacrificed in some form or another to get me to where I am... people like my cousins Dudda, Thunder, Felecia, Wanda, Twuan, and my friends Eric and Carlos. Thank you to the man who stepped in and fathered me through many years of my childhood, Anthony Eleby. I could go on and on.

One person that I can't close without mentioning is the only woman besides my momma and Granny who has loved me despite all my flaws, my wife, Tameka Tyler. I thank God that He has turned this chaos we lived into a story of redemption that will possibly help change someone's life. I love you, Woman, and thank you for not giving up on me!

I have to give a special thanks to Michelle Murray for the hours she spent editing this book so it would make sense to people who are in different places in life. THANKS, MICHELLE!

CHAPTER 1
DIRT ROAD

I often have this thought or vision, I have even dreamed it before, that a faceless person walks up to me and shoots me in the face. When it happens, I'm not scared; I don't die. A few times I've even felt real pain in the spot where I get shot. I used to believe that God was a chess player sitting in heaven, waiting to knock this king over for all of the rooks I'd taken out and all of queens I'd hurt. I used to believe that the shot to the head in my dream was God's checkmate, a strategic move by the cosmic champion. As I had heard 100 times before, it would be me reaping what I had sown. People say that life is like a game of cards, and you have to play the hand that you're dealt. I'd rather say that life is like a movie. We all have a role, and this is mine.

Until the late eighties, my family lived on the remains of an old slave plantation called Bell Chase, in Minter City, Mississippi. It was just like one you'd see in the movies—long, winding dirt road, rows of wood and tin houses, white wooden church at the end of the road, the big white house at the beginning, and cotton fields as far as your eyes could see. When slavery ended in the south, a lot slaves didn't know how to pick up and move on, so they stayed on the plantations as sharecroppers. My family was descendants of that. Minter City was an unincorporated area in Leflore County, the home of T.Y. Fleming High School, the great Olympic basketball player Lucy Harris and, if you didn't know by now, me—Travis Tyler, a.k.a. Thi'sl. I was born into a family of eleven. My granddaddy, Samuel "Dipper" Billingsley, and my grandma, Edna "Bee" Billingsley, had nine kids, one of which is my momma, Reba Tyler.

It was a few days before spring when I was born on March 17. Records show it was 4:40 a.m. when I entered this world. I wish I could tell you some great story about me being born and how I saw the light when I was coming out of the womb, as I thought to myself, in my infant mind, *Look out world, here I come!* But, just like everybody else, I don't remember a thing about being born. What I do know is that I was born at Greenwood Leflore Hospital, a doctor name Crick delivered me, and my granny would not let my daddy in the delivery room because he wasn't married to my momma. I've never asked my momma if she was scared when she was delivering me, but I can only imagine that she was, still a kid herself. That March morning she was only 17 years old, just days away from turning 18 and a couple of months away from graduating high school. Now here she was in a cold hospital room, pushing out a seven-pound baby boy. I came out feet first; not literally, but as soon as my feet hit the ground I was gone. My momma told me that I never even crawled. When I was 8 months old, I was in my swing when it broke. I fell out, landed on my feet, and started walking.

My stay on Bell Chase was short-lived. When I was two, my grandparents packed up a U-Haul truck, piled their kids into a car, and our next stop was St. Louis, Missouri.

My momma was crushed. Not only was she leaving all her friends, but also she was leaving my daddy and taking his son to another state. Richard Spurlock, that's my daddy—one of the coolest, smoothest dudes on the planet. My daddy had style, charisma, all of that. I bet he used some of that to get Momma. My daddy's side of the family tree had a lot of fruit on it too; my granddaddy, Jeff Spurlock, and my grandma, Emma, had eleven kids, including my daddy. I could only imagine my daddy and his side of the family didn't want me to move to another city, but they had no control over it. I was gone.

Our first stop in St. Louis was on the west side, at an apartment building called The Martanna, owned by my granddaddy's brother, James. Back on Bell Chase, my granddaddy worked for the plantation owner, Mr. Billie, operating heavy machinery. When Uncle James started his company, Billingsley Construction, my grandpa moved up to run it for him. Uncle James had moved to St. Louis years before we did, with the dream of building a life for his family. He came with nothing, got hired at General Motors, worked hard, saved money, bought The Martanna (a six-family apartment building), and started his company. He bought The Martanna so his mother—my great grandmother, Maude Billingsley (Big Momma)—and the rest of our family would have somewhere to stay when they came from Mississippi.

My Grandma Bee was always like my second momma. Everyone knew she loved her grandson. When my momma had me she was a senior in high school, so my granny watched me like her own until my momma graduated. When we moved to St. Louis, my momma immediately found a job and started working, so of course while she was at work, I was with Granny. Up until I was five years old, I was my momma's only child and my grandma's only grandchild, but that all changed when my little brother Shawn was born. My momma always worked a lot, and when she wasn't working, she was out kicking it. That meant Shawn and I spent a lot of time with Grandma Bee.

We often made trips back to Bell Chase to visit our family still there. One of the most memorable visits was the summer I turned seven; it was the first time I met my cousin Alfreddie Randall, a.k.a. Tank. Most of that day is sketchy in my brain, but the things I do remember are golden. We were in front of my Auntie Bert's house, playing in a puddle of muddy water, while my momma and Tank's momma, Maudie B., were in the house hanging out. From the jump, we clicked! Tank and I were the same age, but he was four months older. Even though technically he was the older cousin, I was bigger than him. We played out front for what seemed like forever. My time with my new road dawg was short-lived, because I had to go back to St. Louis and I guess he had to go back to Chicago where they lived. Back in St. Louis, I got a surprise that I definitely wasn't expecting...Tank and his family were at Big Momma's house!

One of the best things about living in a six-family apartment building with all of your family had to be that it was like having your own gang. The Billingsleys...well my last name was Tyler, and Tank's was Randall...but we were still Billingsleys and we were deep. At the grade school alone there were nine of us: me, Tank, Fee, Dudda, Tonya (a.k.a. Thunder), Angie (Geece), my little brother, plus two of our other little cousins, Brian and Stephanie. Added on top of our nine, we had all of our friends from our street too. We were like twenty-deep, and that was just at the grade school. The numbers didn't stop there with us either—we had cousins at the middle school and at the high school. We really were our own gang.

Every day after school we did the same thing—rushed straight to Big Momma's house. In the words of my big cousin Ortez, "Second floor east is where we feast," and that we did every day. We'd get our plates and sit in front of the TV, on the living room floor. Big Momma had those plates going like an assembly line…always a table full of plates, and whatever the kids didn't get, the grownups did. The only times this routine was interrupted was the first of the month and report card day. The first of the month was like a holiday! When you're on welfare, once all of the money is gone and the food stamps are gone, the rest of the month is usually a struggle. There's no choice of food, no shopping, and if somebody gets high or drunk, that's even worse. So, the first of the month was like FEMA relief. On the first, it was popping!

Now, report card day was another story. If the first of the month was like a holiday, then report card day was like judgment day. I was a straight-A student, but I had certain family members that could not get it right in school, and they would experience what we called a "stretching." A stretching is when one person takes your legs, another takes your wrists, and they hold you face down on the floor while somebody whoops you with a belt. Those things were serious! I only got stretched one time in elementary and the crazy thing was, it was because I had one bad grade, the rest were A's.

I was always real smart in school; there was nothing in school that I didn't understand. My momma said I got that from my daddy's side of the family. My teachers called my momma to the school for a meeting when I was still in elementary and asked her to let them put me up some grades. My momma wasn't too long out of the country, so she didn't understand the type of opportunity that was for me. She told them no.

I have never had the desire to play any sports, but I was academically competitive. Learning was my sport. If there was a kid in my class even close to being as smart as I was, I wanted to beat them. If they got an A, I wanted an A+. One of my favorite classes in elementary was Learning Enrichment, because I loved writing. I had a passion for writing, and according to my Learning Enrichment teacher, Mrs. Crockett, I had a gift to write. She'd praise and encourage me to write about different experiences. One year I got some sad news that inspired me to write something that led to one of the most memorable moments of my life. The news was that my Grandfather Jeff had a stroke and the writing was a book called "My Grandfather and I."

Before my granddaddy had a stroke, I didn't know what they were and the way people explained it to me didn't help me understand it either. It wasn't until I went to see Grandpa Jeff that I learned how serious a stroke was. In my childhood mind, Grandpa Jeff was the epitome of strength and of what a man should be. He was 6-foot-4 or so, 250+ pounds, but stocky from years of manual labor in the old Mississippi. Looking up at him when I was a child was like looking up at a tree or a giant; he used to lift me over his head with no effort. I will never forget walking in to that hospital to see my papa. It was dull, like they had green lights instead of really white ones, and the smell…it smelled like *sick*. The elevator ride up was the longest three floors ever. When the door opened up, it was scary! First thing I saw was a man in a wheelchair with his head hanging to one side, wearing a hospital gown and socks, moving in slow motion. There was a TV room full of people, dressed the same as he was, just sitting there staring at the screen. I made it to my grandpa's room as fast as I could. When I got to his room, I was faced with a big surprise, because the man in that bed was not my Papa Jeff. The sign outside the door had his name on it, the chart had his name on it, and my Grandma Emma even said his name, but the man lying in that bed wasn't the papa I knew. He lay there looking close to lifeless from the neck down; from the neck up he was almost drooling, and he couldn't talk clearly. The tree of a man I knew had been chopped down.

When I walked in, my grandma was excited to see me, and I could tell she knew I was caught off-guard by how Grandpa looked. "Jeff, Jeff, do you know who this is, Jeff?" Grandma Emma asked him, hoping he would know. I was scared to hear his answer. I thought he wouldn't remember me, especially since he didn't look like himself. We all stood there looking and waiting to see if he remembered me, and then after working up the strength, he spoke slowly, with his teary eyes fixed on me, "Travis." Whew, I was relieved! I stood in there most of my visiting time, trying to wrap my eight-year-old mind around how this thing called a stroke had stripped my granddaddy of his super powers. What was this stroke? How did he catch it? Could my other grandpa get it? Could kids get it? Would he get rid of it? I didn't know what it was, but I knew it had to be tough to do my papa like that, so I was scared of "strokes."

Back at school, we had a special assignment in Learning Enrichment; we had to write a book. Mrs. Crockett told us to write about something that meant a lot to us, and after coming back from seeing my grandpa, the only thing that was on my mind was him and that stroke, so that's what I wrote about. I started out talking about the things Grandpa and I used to do when I would visit, like him pretending to let me drive. I went on to talk about how I found out he had the stroke and how it made me feel when my momma told me. Mrs. Crockett was over my shoulder every week, checking what I was writing. By the time I was halfway through it, she was more excited than I was about it. When I finished, she had me rewrite the words in my best handwriting and draw the best pictures I could, then I turned it in. The next week when we came back to class, Mrs. Crockett gave me the book back, but it wasn't the one I gave her. It looked better. She had taken the pages I gave her, laminated them, and put a black plastic spiral holder through it. It looked like a book; I was speechless. The news she gave us after that made us all even more excited. She told us that all of our books were going to be in this event called the Young Authors' Book Fair.

The Young Authors' Book Fair was held at Harris Stowe State College, and there were books submitted from students all over St. Louis, grades K-12. It was a Saturday morning, the sun was shining bright, and the weather was perfect for the bus ride my Grandma Bee, my brother, and I were about to take. I was so excited, but it was one of those bittersweet things. I was excited, but my momma or my daddy wasn't there, so I was a little hurt. My daddy hadn't ever been to anything of mine, so even though it hurt, I was used to it. My momma had to work, as usual. I wanted her to be there so badly, but I knew her working was what kept new shoes on my feet and our bills paid, so I understood.

Walking up to Harris-Stowe campus was some kind of feeling. This was the biggest school I had ever seen! We walked up some giant steps…they were like steps to a palace or something, not a school. My anxiety rose higher and higher with every step; I didn't know what to expect. When we walked into the auditorium, there were books and people everywhere. We walked around for a good twenty minutes before I saw something that caught my eye—the refreshment table. We walked around looking at books for a while before a woman started speaking on stage. "I know her, Grandma,"

I told my grams between bites of my cookies. The woman's name was Jane; she was a storyteller who came to our school and read books to our class. Everyone in the room stopped and listened as she passionately talked about the importance of reading. She went on and on about it, and then in the middle of her talking, she switched the subject. She said, "Out of all the books in here today, there was one that stood out to me above them all. I want to take the time right now to read it." Before she said that, she was losing me…like I said she was going on and on. When she started reading the book, it instantly caught my attention. My head snapped up from my daydreaming, and so I wouldn't break the silence of the room, I whispered to my grandma, "That's my book she's reading!" My grandma looked at me and said, "Shhh!" I said again, a little bit louder this time, "No, Grandma, for real, that's my book she's reading!"

As she finished reading, Jane said, "The name of the book is 'My Grandfather and I,' written by Travis Tyler. I would like to call him up. Travis, if you're here, come on up!" I looked at my grams and said, "I told you, Grandma, she was reading my book." I went up to the stage, and the lady continued on to say how much she loved my book and how well I had written it being so young. She shook my hand, so I shook hers, but not before taking a bite of one of my cookies.

My momma was so proud of me about that book. She told everyone. She even called Mississippi and told my daddy. I mean it was some kind of a big deal, I guess. Out of thousands of books in that auditorium that day, from different kids at different schools, she had chosen and read mine.

Before the trip to see my Grandpa Jeff, I had only seen my daddy one time since we moved to St. Louis. He came up to visit us, and the only thing I remember about the visit was going to see my mom at work. He did send me a bike for Christmas when I was seven, and man did I love that bike. My momma felt like I needed to go see my daddy, so that summer she sent me to Mississippi. Grandma Bee wasn't too thrilled about it, but I was. It didn't matter to me how many birthdays he missed, Christmases, any of that, I loved my daddy and wanted to see him. My Grandma Emma and Grandpa Jeff had since moved from Minter City on Bell Chase; they lived in Greenwood now. My Auntie Bert, Grandma Bee's sister, lived in Greenwood, too, right around the corner from my daddy. Knowing that made my Grandma Bee feel a little bit better.

Greenwood is the "city" like St. Louis…well, it's in the country and the people were "country," but it looked like the city. One thing was for sure; it was a lot different from Bell Chase. The closer I got to my daddy's house, the more my anxiety built up. I had this whole idea in my head of how it would play out, because I just knew he missed me as much as I missed him. We turned into their neighborhood, and I started counting the houses before we arrived. One, two, three, we pulled into my granny's driveway and there I was. I got out of the car and strolled up the narrow concrete walkway with a stomach full of butterflies. I was nervous because I hadn't seen all of them since I was two years old, so I had no clue what kind of people I'd be spending my summer break with.

I had an idea in my little eight-year-old brain of what I thought the summer break would be like. My daddy and I would have so much fun because he was going to be so excited to finally spend time with me. It would be non-stop, over the top fun, father and son summertime fun. I couldn't wait, but when I got there, my dad wasn't nearly as excited as I thought he would be. He was actually asleep. My daddy was a security guard at Parson State Prison, and his schedule went as such: he worked all night, slept most of the day, woke up, got ready for work, and left. The two days he had off during the week were usually spent at his girlfriend's house; she also worked at the prison and had the same schedule.

What that meant for me was the same thing it meant in St. Louis—while my parent worked, I was with my grandparent. My Grandma Emma and my Grandma Bee were two totally different people, though. My Grandma Bee had quiet strength, but you knew she could handle things, anything if needed. She worked hard, kept money, dressed nice, and went to church faithfully. My Grandma Emma, on the other hand, was a different story. She loved Tab sodas, cigarettes, and soap operas…and you better be quiet while she was watching them. Grandma Emma also loved playing bingo, and in a way she was a straight hustler. Grandma Emma gave me the lowdown on how to pull off one of the first schemes I ever did.

It was a hot, sunny day…M–I–crooked letter hot, and I needed something to cool me off. Every neighborhood has a candy lady, and there the candy lady lived right around the corner from my granny. She sold ices (frozen Kool-Aid cups). She had 10-cent ices in small Styrofoam cups and 25-cent ices in bigger cups. This particular day, as badly as I wanted an icy, I was broke and Grandma Emma was broke, too. My granny had these bracelets that she used to wear around her ankles with coins as decorations. On this particular day, she told me to get one of her bracelets, then to go outside and get some tar off the ground outside. Granny took a coin off of her bracelet and stuffed the piece of tar into the hole that was holding the coin onto the bracelet. She then instructed me to ask for a 10-cent icy, pay with the coin, and walk off. I thought to myself, *This won't be too hard. By the time she notices the dime, I'll be long gone, and she'll never know who did it.*

I made it to the candy lady's house, took the coin out of my pocket, and knocked on the door. Candy Lady came to the door as normal, asked me what I wanted, and went inside to get it. She came back with my icy—my red Kool-Aid icy. All I was thinking about was flipping it upside down and eating it. She handed me my icy, I checked it out to make sure the product was cool, then I handed her the dime. To my surprise, she didn't look at it immediately. She took it, turned around, and closed her door. I walked off the porch smiling hard! I wasn't halfway down the block when I heard the candy lady yelling at me. "HEY, HEY, THIS DIME HAS A HOLE IN IT!" She caught me! There was no way, as hot as it was, that I was giving that icy back, so I did the first thing that came to mind. I took off running and didn't look back.

Every opportunity I had to be with my daddy, I took it, even if it was five minutes. One of the best things my daddy ever showed me in my life only lasted about five minutes, but it awakened something rooted deep inside of me that would eventually change my life. One afternoon as we were sitting around the house, my daddy took me to the back room that my Auntie Renee slept in. I didn't have a clue what was going on, but I was interested to see. The only things that were in Auntie Renee's room were a bed, a window, and this old dusty piano. My daddy sat down on the bench, looked at me and asked, "Do you like music? Let me show you something." He lifted his hands, put them to the worn ivory keys, stepped his fingers across them with such precision, and something inside me was lit. The melody wasn't that complex; it was the sound of the piano keys falling that captured me and made me want to create something just as beautiful. I spent a lot of days in there after that, trying to teach myself how to play.

The most I came up with was random melodies and "Mary Had a Little Lamb." Music had found its way into my heart, or maybe it had found its way out of my heart. All I knew was that I wanted to be close to it. I found so much peace sitting there day after day, trying to create some beautiful music of my own.

I wish I could tell you that everything I learned in that room was just as beautiful, but it wasn't. The same way that in less than five minutes a few simple keys from an old piano had awakened something beautiful in me, I was awakened to other things in that room that weren't so beautiful. The setting was the same as the day my daddy took me in there and showed me the piano, except for two differences. One, this time it was night. Two, the teacher was not my dad; the teacher was my thirteen-year-old uncle. We went in the room and sat down on the bed. It didn't seem too strange at first. My uncle went to the closet and pulled something out of a bag, then sat down beside me. He turned to me and asked, "Have you ever smelled a girl? Do you know what a woman smells like?" Of course, my answer was, "No." I was eight years old; I didn't even know what he was talking about. That's when he showed me what he had pulled out the closet…it was a pair of panties. He put them up to his nose, breathed in deep, and said, "That's what girl smells like." Then he put it to my nose and said, "Smell it; smells good, doesn't it?" Here I was in the same room where I had just been turned on to beautiful melody, and now I had a deep-seated feeling again; but this one was not awakening as with music. When I heard the keys falling on that piano, it was like a light came on. This didn't feel like that. It didn't feel like a light, it almost felt dirty, but it definitely turned something on.

I looked forward to the weekends because my daddy was off work, and if I was lucky I'd get some time to hang with him. One weekend, our hanging turned out to have a pretty good surprise involved. My daddy got up much earlier than he usually would after work, and as soon as he got up, we hit the road. After driving for a couple of hours, according to the signs, we had arrived in Ackerman, Mississippi. We pulled in front of a house and got out of the car. Before we made it to the gate, a woman that my daddy called "Judy" greeted us. She was real friendly towards me, like she had heard of me before but hadn't ever seen me. We walked into the house to a front room full of people. It was obvious they knew my daddy because they called him by name. "Hey, Richard!" rang out all over the room, in many different country accents. Then this little girl that looked to be around three years old ran up to my daddy and hugged his legs super hard. My daddy hugged her back, looked at me, and said, "This is your little sister, Sonya. Surprise!" A surprise it definitely was, and I didn't have any time to process it to really see how I felt. She was the cutest little thing, though. Her little blue jean shorts and t-shirt were neat, and her hair was combed to perfection, braided out with beads on it. I fell in love with her instantly. Every step I took that day, she was right behind me. She obviously was just as happy that I was her big brother as I was that she was my little sister. Sadly, the joy we felt that day would end with both of us in tears as she watched Daddy and me drive off.

Some of the most memorable moments of that summer were cracking jokes for my Grandpa Jeff. His stroke still had him off his feet and he could only do a few things by himself. My granny still had to feed him and wash him, because he couldn't move his arms the same, but the things he could do, he didn't want any help. That stroke had lamed his body, but it couldn't kill the man that my grandpa was on the inside. Once he was helped out of his bed, he would get himself down the hall in that wheelchair with all he had in him. You could hear him coming out of that room, wheels turning and feet dragging, as he made his way to the living room.

His favorite TV show was Gomer Pyle. Man, he loved that show. He would laugh so hard when Gomer Pyle would say, "Surprise, Surprise, Surprise!" I could only imagine how my grandpa felt—once a giant of a man, provider for his family, lover to his wife, hard-working man of the field, and now all of his strength and wisdom were trapped inside a body he couldn't control, not even enough to speak clearly. It had to be hard. Some days I could see the pain in his eyes and tell he was sad, and every time I saw it, I would look at him and say, "Surprise, Surprise, Surprise!" He would laugh so hard.

I loved being in Mississippi with my family, but I was so homesick I didn't know what to do. So, what I decided to do was call people I knew in St. Louis. What I didn't know was that it cost money to call another state. I talked my granny's phone bill up so high that month that she wanted to kill me! The end of the summer couldn't come fast enough. I liked Mississippi, but I loved being at home in St. Louis more, and there were a lot of things different from home. At home, especially at my Grandma Bee's house, I could have almost anything I wanted. Down here, because there were so many people in the house, sometimes I couldn't get the type of food I wanted. I knew whenever it got too bad, all I had to do was hop on the phone and call my Grandma Bee, and she would make sure I was cool. My gram's sister, Bertha, or Auntie Bert as we called her, lived right around the corner from my Grandma Emma and Grandpa Jeff. All I had to do was call Grandma Bee, she would call Auntie Bert, then I would walk over there to get money and food. My Grandma Emma was classic. Every time I got back from my Auntie

Bert's house, she knew I had money, and I knew she would say the same thing—"Baby, I know you're going to buy your grandma a Tab and some cigarettes." It never failed.

Not having food wasn't my biggest problem that summer. By far, it was the things my uncle was teaching me, trying to get me to do, or trying to do to me when no one else was around. My uncle had a friend who was just as perverted as he was, and that friend had a little sister the same age as me, eight. My uncle, in his perverted mind, thought his homeboy's little sister would be a good person for me to put into practice the stuff he had been talking to me about. So he told me to make her my girlfriend. At this point, I'd had only one girlfriend ever, in a grade school understanding of the word. You know how it is—you're in class or on the schoolyard and see the cute girl...the one whose barrettes match her socks and shirt. You tell your friends, they make fun of you, they tell her, she smiles at you, and with nothing more than a two-second smile confirmation, she is your girlfriend. At least, until her mom finds the notes in her book bag that you've been writing her. Before then, that was the only idea I had of a girlfriend, but my uncle felt it was time to bring all of the stuff he was showing me to life. It ended up looking like this: midday, my girlfriend and I were locked in a side room. I went in there with a head full of instructions from my uncle of what and how I should do things. I didn't know what to expect from this at all, and she probably felt the same. Needless to say, nothing much happened...we were eight years old. We spent the next hour trying to kiss while failing horribly, which was very disappointing to my uncle. In the midst of that situation, I had two strong conflicting feelings going on in me at one time. One, I was anxious and filled with this burning excitement. Two, whenever I would stop long enough to think about what I was doing, I would be consumed by this stomach-crunching, dirty feeling. My uncle, on the other hand, wished that I had gone further. Who gets a kick out of seeing two eight-year-olds locked in a room, attempting to have sex? He did, apparently. He even had a thing for eight-year-olds, or at least he couldn't make up his mind whether he liked little boys, a.k.a. me, or girls. More than once, he tried to get me to do things, and if it wasn't for my Uncle Keith, he may have succeeded.

My joy about being in Greenwood for the summer had come and gone. The person I was there to see didn't have time to spend with me at all, so I was long overdue for a car ride back to St. Louis. I had just about taken all I could take of Old Miss, and I was ready to go. So, I thought up a good plan to get me out of there real fast. I wrote a note that said something like, "I'm tired of being here, I want to go home and nobody will let me, so I am running away to the swimming pool to drown myself." I put the note on the washer and hid in the closet under some clothes all afternoon. I could hear everyone looking for me, walking through the house calling my name, "TRAVIS!!!" I would hear them leave, and then come back in. Sometime later, someone would say, "I've been to the store, he wasn't there," and, 'I've been here and there…he wasn't there.' After a while, for some reason, I remember just giving up and coming out. Maybe I was hungry, maybe I was tired, hot, I don't know, but I came out. As I came out of hiding, my Uncle Keith was coming back in the house, and he was heated. Since the note said I was going to drown myself, Keith took it literally, as he should have, because I could have been floating face down in a pool. So, I am glad he went looking for me, but the problem was, it was over 90 degrees, the pool was across the tracks, and he walked. Man, he came in that door looking like he had been out in a cotton field all day. He was sweating badly! When he found out I had been in the house hiding, he whooped me super hard with his hand. Everybody in the whole house was heated at me, but the good thing for me was that it was enough to get me home. When my daddy found out what happened, he basically had the attitude of *whatever*. He felt like if I wanted to get out of there that badly, then I should go, and I couldn't agree more. I mean, I loved my family down there, and I would miss my grandparents, but I wanted to get home!

Soon, I was in the back seat of a car headed back to St. Louis. I had a lot good adventures that summer. I met my little sister for the first time, had a lot of fun moments with my Grandpa Jeff, and kicked it with my Uncle Keith, but that wasn't enough to make me want to stay. Driving back to St. Louis, I thought about my daddy a lot. No matter what, I loved my daddy, and I was hurt that I didn't get to spend a lot of time with him. He was the person I'd come to see.

CHAPTER 2
WESTSIDE STORY

"Welcome to Missouri." I was SOOOOOOO happy to see that sign and the arch. YES, I was home! I made it home a couple of weeks before school started, right in time for one of my favorite events—BACK TO SCHOOL SHOPPING! I missed my momma when she worked all the time, but one of the benefits of that was she bought us close to everything we wanted. Shawn was only four; he didn't need much, so that made it even better for me. Plus, his daddy, James, was there with us, and he bought me stuff too. My aunties, especially Jackie, bought me stuff, and my granny took me riding with her every weekend and bought me stuff. Life was good!

The Saturday morning haircut right before the first day of school was a ritual that heightened the anticipation. I knew after the haircut, the only things between school and me were Saturday afternoon and Sunday. Besides the joy of waking up and putting on all this new stuff—shirt, shoes, pants, socks, and even belt—there was the ever-present anxiety of change. We're coming from almost three months away from school. We would have a new teacher, at least those of us who passed. People got taller, smaller, hair grew, hair cut, girls got cute, and dudes got tougher, all of that had happened in a matter of three months. The anxiety came from wondering, *where will I fit in to the equation?* I loved school and couldn't wait to start fourth grade.

We were too deep; it was still like we had our own gang. At one point there were fifteen of us at the same school, all cousins. This year, our numbers declined because a couple of our cousins went to the neighborhood middle school, Cook Middle, and the family was deep there, too. Every day after school, we still walked straight to The Martanna and straight to Big Momma's house. As sure as the clock hand struck 3:00 every day, it never failed—she would have plates all around the table. My brother and I would stay on Maple every day until my momma got off work. She didn't have to worry about having someone watching us, because everybody in the building was family, so we were good. Once we finished eating, we hit the living room to watch cartoons or we went straight outside. The front porch at The Martanna was the hangout spot for the whole block. There was always somebody out there, especially if it was the "first of the month."

Any day of the week, the porch would have a gang of people on it, but on Saturdays and on the first, it would be super packed. First of the month, it got started early, especially if it was a weekend. As soon as people's eyes opened, it was off to the porch to wait on the mailman bringing the checks and food stamps. We had a corner store in our hood that even gave out credit and sold beer on food stamps; they just charged double. So if the mailman ran late, my people would hit the store and get some beers to knock off while they waited on the mailman, to get the party started. For the most part, my momma always kept a job, but even though she worked, she would still be on the porch kicking it hard. McDonald's always seemed to be the fast food of choice, and trips to the corner store were frequent. The more kids you had, the more you got with food stamps, but the welfare check was never enough to live off of. I never really understood welfare growing up; all I knew was once a month it brought joy to my life. Until I got older and understood it better, I thought welfare was only for poor black people in the hood, because growing up that's all I saw on it. I remember my aunties used to joke and say that the money and food stamps were from our daddy, "The President." As exciting as welfare was on the first of the month, it was just as depressing for some for the rest of the month, because it was gone as fast as it came.

In 1985, a parent with two children, getting welfare, would receive around $285 cash a month and maybe $350 worth of food stamps. There was no way possible to support three people with $285 a month. That's why it brought joy for the day, but for the month, that joy didn't last. Even with the hustle of selling food stamps for cash ($65 book for $40 cash), you would still come up short. The dilemma would then be "I paid my bills, but now we can't eat." Even with my momma working a job, there were times we still would have to get food stamps. Her job just didn't always make enough to support the three of us. But when job, welfare checks, and food stamps didn't add up, we had something else that came through—the church up the street!

The church gave out food every other Wednesday and they had a gym they let us hoop in every Friday. Now, it wasn't like the church was handing out T-bone steaks, but the box that they did give you was like a "ghetto survival kit." Every now and then, you'd get lucky and receive a box of cake mix or something special, but that was mainly around the holidays. What you knew would be in there every time: a box of powdered milk, some off-brand cereal, boxes of macaroni with the powder cheese mix, plenty of cans of green beans, plenty of corn, and a block of American cheese in that rectangular brown box. That cheese was thick and hard to cut, but we loved it! I used to try to slice that stuff and messed it up every time. One end would be all skinny and the other end would be super wide. We would be in the kitchen, trying to make cheese toast and grilled cheese, always burning up one end because the cheese wouldn't melt. My cousin Ortez—that's Dudda's big brother, he was older than all of us—he used to get his cut perfect every time. He was the king at cutting that cheese block.

One thing about The Martanna was that we were not alone in our struggles and struggling together made us closer, at least the kids. When our mommas were all hanging out together in the neighborhood lounge on the weekends, we were all hanging out together. Our Friday nights usually consisted of the same thing: playing on the porch until the parents left, playing in the hall once they were gone, and finally, the main event... Friday Night Videos! We would be standing in front of the TV, singing and dancing to Michael Jackson, George Michaels, Culture Club, Herbie Hancock, and whatever else they played. At that moment, no problems existed and everything was good.

When you walked up the steps to the third floor, the corners and the ceilings went up real high. We would beat box in the corner, making music with our mouths. Ortez made up a rap song about The Martanna, and it was a must that he said it every time we hit the hall. The designated beat boxer would get in their corner; Ortez would get in his corner and start his rap. "M. A. R. T. A. N. N. A, Maple Boulevard is where I stay. Second floor east is where I feast..." He would go on and talk about our aunts, and rap about stuff you would only know if you were from Maple. Seeing the way everybody in the hallway got hype made me want to rap! But I don't think anything or anybody made me want to be a rapper more than LL Cool J. I remember listening to *I'm Bad* and feeling like I could do anything! I wanted to rock a Kangol, I wanted the troop jacket, and I actually had the troop shoes. I remember everybody would swap the line out on *I'm Bad* and fill in their own name. "So forget Oreos, eat ＿＿＿＿＿＿ ＿＿＿＿＿＿ cookies. I'm bad!"

Everybody on earth loves some form of music. Whether it's blue grass, country, rock, house, orchestra, whatever kind, somebody loves it. It was one thing to watch Friday Night Videos and see George Michaels singing, "You've got to have faith…" or Michael Jackson singing *Billy Jean*, and get hype. I loved it, it made me want to move, but I couldn't fully relate. It wasn't my heartbeat; it wasn't my pulse. It didn't have the intensity and aggression of my everyday living environment but rap did, and from the first time I heard it I fell in love with it. It understood me. It told my story. It was my voice. By sixth grade year, rap music had become "the voice of the street." You heard it everywhere! People would be playing it on their porches, in the house, in their cars, on headphones, house parties, everywhere.

Have you ever heard of the "Westside Rockers?" It may sound familiar to you because of the ring it has to it. It could have been the name of an old Negro league team, or a jazz band or something, but it wasn't. The Westside Rockers was the neighborhood gang, and anyone would argue that the leader was a 14-year-old kid named Johnny Filmore. Johnny was fourteen, but he wasn't a little dude. He was cut for being that young, about 6-feet tall, and everybody knew he had no problem putting his hands on someone if he needed to. I once saw him hit a dude for trying to talk to his girlfriend. It was like a movie! When he hit that boy, dude came off the ground, flew into the fence, then his feet were already running when he hit the ground. To this day, that dude still has a black mark under his eye from that one punch. Johnny's girlfriend at the time was my cousin, Felecia, arguably the co-leader of her own gang (along with her sister, Rochelle), "The Westside Possettes." They were girls, but the same rules applied. Everybody knew that they would put their hands on you if need be. They had a gang of cute girls that had no problem fighting anybody. Tank and I were the two youngest dudes hanging around The Rockers besides our boy, Sweet Pea, Johnny's little brother.

Tank and I didn't have any big brothers or daddies around, so Johnny and the rest of the big homies—Wayne, Fox, Oscar, Norris, Gus, Leo, PMD—they were our big brothers. We had a summer camp at Forest Park Community College that used to pick kids up in our hood every summer. I remember a time I was on the bus, and a dude way older than me was showing out big time for this girl. He was going in on me, talking bad, big talk. Truthfully, I wasn't scared of him; I just knew I wouldn't win. The stuff he said wasn't really bothering or getting to me, what he was saying wasn't hurting my feelings, but it was making me mad that I couldn't do anything to stop him. All I kept telling him was "Keep talking, wait until I tell my big brothers." Of course, because he was showing out for the girls, he wouldn't shut up. But when I mentioned my "big brothers," I saw fear in his eyes. When I made it back to the hood and told Johnny what happened, all he said was, "For real, I got you." The next day, dude was on the same mission again, talking crazy to me. This time I wasn't mad at all. I just laughed, because I knew he wouldn't be talking for too much longer. As the bus rounded the corner at Horton Street, he was still talking big! I looked up the street and could see my dudes up the hill, and I knew it was on. I didn't start wilding out with him, or none of that. All I did was say, "Remember I told you about my brothers? That's them." His whole attitude changed then; he started with the "I was just playing"-type stuff. I walked off the bus in front of him, and he acted like he didn't want to get off. As soon as he stepped foot off the bus, I pointed him out, "That's him." Johnny walked over there like, "You was messing with my little brother?" Before the dude could answer, he got one of those punches! Needless to say, I didn't have any more problems out of him or anybody else on that bus.

You can't have a gang like The Westside Rockers or a dude like Johnny around, without somebody bucking up against the system. That's just how it works. If everybody's going around saying this dude is the hardest dude on the west side, there will be somebody else that feels the same way about themselves or their squad. And, if those two people are too close in proximity, the chances are they will be enemies before friends. In this case, that person was Dorsey Brandon and his gang was called, "The B.O.D." (The Boys of Destruction). Dorsey and Johnny were alike in a lot of ways, even down to their looks. They went after the same girls and were even the same age. The first time I ever heard about Dorsey was at a house party Johnny threw at his momma's house. The B.O.D. came over there deep. They sent two dudes that nobody would recognize to the door first, to peep out the scene, and then they all tried to come in. I remember the person answering the door saying that The B.O.D. were at the door. Next thing I knew, the whole hood was mobbing out the door, chasing them back across Page Avenue.

My momma worked hard all the time, but we were not getting all the stuff we were used to. Every now and then, we would end up living with one of my family members— aunts, uncles, cousins—and it would usually end in an argument of some sort between the adults, then we would leave. We stayed with my Auntie Shea more than anybody else, because her and my momma usually got along the best. They had their times when they would argue, but they were cool overall. My Auntie Shea had four kids, my momma had two, and with their two boyfriends in the house, that made ten people in one spot. Usually when we stayed together, it would be in a two-bedroom apartment. Even when it was a three-bedroom, there were just too many of us. One time, we lived in Maplewood (St. Louis County), and there were actually sixteen of us staying in a three-bedroom apartment. Every room in that house was full—the only thing empty most times in the house was the refrigerator. If it weren't for my granny, a lot of days it would have been all-bad.

My mom always worked hard; but as we grew older, no matter how much she worked, it wasn't enough. The times when it wasn't enough, though, Momma always made a way, and that made me love her even more. I remember one day in particular we were all hungry and my momma only had $5 to her name. We had no food in the house at all, so Momma went to White Castle to get some burgers. I sat there and watched my momma spend her last $5 on food, and she didn't take a bite. She gave every one of those burgers to my brother and me without thinking twice. Another time, it was blazing hot in the summer and we didn't have AC. We lay on the floor together, and momma put the only fan we had on my brother and me. Her boyfriend tried to turn it to them, but Momma would have none of that.

My daddy, on the other hand…even though I loved him as much as any son does their father, he wasn't as much of a hero to me as my momma was. Every month my momma got a $50 check from my daddy for child support, and in most cases she just used it on me. No matter how it went, $50 wasn't enough to support me. I don't know how much money they were taking from my daddy, but all we got was $50. One day I walked to the pay phone to call my daddy, trying to get him to send me some money because we didn't have a thing to eat. His response was something like, "Didn't your momma get that money this month?" Our conversation ended shortly after that, with no promise of assistance and me walking back home still hungry.

No matter what my daddy did, I never hated him. I was hurt, but I still loved him. I actually used to think he was going to come and rescue me from my situation and be the hero I always wanted him to be, but he never did. One year, on my birthday, I sat looking out our window all day, because for some strange reason I thought my birthday was so important to him that he would pop up. But he didn't. My momma knew I was waiting on my daddy to show up, but she also knew that he would never come. To make me feel better, she told me the bike she bought was from him. Man, I loved that bike! I would have loved that bike from anybody, but I loved that bike because I thought it came from my daddy. I rode that thing for hours, until it got dark, and the next day I did it again. Years later, I was crushed when I found out that my daddy didn't send me that bike. Momma made the story up because she knew I was missing him, and she knew that would make me feel better.

If Momma really wanted to make me happy, then she wouldn't have been gone so much. I understood she had to work, but when she wasn't working, she would still be gone with her friends or boyfriend. My momma mostly hung around with the same group of people all the time. Momma was social, but she wasn't a friendly bob that brought new friends or random men home. On paydays, if she wasn't out kicking it, she would be at the house with her crew. If that was the case, either she would be in the living room while we were in our room, or closed-off in her room. The scene was always the same: minimal light, music playing in the background (usually Anita Baker or Teena Marie), four or five people, drinks, and clouds of smoke. When I say clouds of smoke, I'm not talking about cigarette smoke, even though for a long time I thought that's what it was. I knew it smelled different than cigarettes, but I didn't know what kind of smoke it was. After the weekend gatherings were over, I would sneak out to see what, or *who* in some cases, would be lying around. The paraphernalia was usually the same. I would find empty beer bottles, full ashtrays, and these little yellow bags that looked like small mailing envelopes. They would usually have little seeds in them that smelled just like the smoke clouds. I didn't know what they were, but I knew that every weekend Momma and her friends had them on deck. I later found out that weed came in those bags and those seeds came with weed.

When my momma wasn't at home, we would either stay with my granny or my Auntie Shea. My granny's house was always the fun spot! She kept food, soda, snacks, and whatever we could want. Her house was dope. On the flip side, my Auntie Shea watching us was a whole different thing. Auntie always seemed to be upset about something, whether it was at her boyfriend or her current situation. Whenever she was upset, it usually ended in me getting a really nice whooping, in most cases for no reason. One time she whooped me so long in the bathroom, I remember crawling under the sink and begging her to stop. "That's enough, you whooped me enough," but that only made her whoop me some more. As she whooped me, she kept saying, "I'll let you know when it's enough!" Here I was again helpless, at the mercy of a person who was supposed to be taking care of me while my parent was gone. When my momma would come back after those types of situations, I wanted to tell her what was going on, but I didn't. My momma should have been able to tell by how happy I was to see her that something was happening while she was gone. Auntie never touched Shawn, though, just me. It made me feel like he was better than me or like I had done something to deserve the punishment. I loved my auntie, but hated the situation.

After that summer in Mississippi, I experimented with sex in some form or fashion, every chance I got. Those experiences that summer opened the door, and finding my mom's boyfriend's porno magazine stash in the bathroom walked me on through it. After looking at those pictures and reading the stories, that burning I felt inside grew much bigger, and I wanted to have sex more than ever. When my momma would leave, or they would be asleep, I would spend hours looking through the books. I was trying to have sex with everyone that I could. My auntie's friend's daughter— she was basically like a live-in; the girl Jackie, that stayed upstairs; this girl Tina, in my class…it didn't matter. I was trying, but wasn't successful, not yet. All the fifth-grade girls were not about that life yet, but the ones that were had no problem with making it known. They would tell the stories about their after school activities better than the dudes. I knew enough from reading those books and talking to people older than me to be in on the conversations, even though I was lying. It made me look a little cooler because nobody knew I was lying. In the stories, I just placed my "girlfriend" in the same place where I put everything else I lied about… my daddy's house. When I came back from summer break and made up dope stories, and people started asking where the stuff was? Oh yeah, it's over at my daddy's house. "Yeah, I have a German shepherd, he's two years old. His name's King." "Where is he?" "Over at my daddy's house." So that was the same place I was having sex. If they only knew, I didn't even know where my daddy lived.

CHAPTER 3
GANG SIGNS

My exit from elementary school was done in a most dramatic fashion, thanks to Hamilton Branch staff. We had this assembly with all of the fifth graders, and at the end they played Whitney Houston's *The Greatest Love of All*, and before I knew it, the entire fifth-grade class was crying. Kids crying, teachers crying, everybody was crying, even me. I didn't know why I was crying though; all I knew was it just felt right. Maybe because the song was so moving, because truth be told, everybody I cared about was walking home with me after school. Well, I did care about my PE teacher. She was one of the few people who cared about me that didn't have to. One day, she took a group of us from the school to Union Station and a St. Louis University basketball game. That day stuck with me all my life. All of my teachers wished me well, though. They knew the potential I had, and they hoped I would use it to succeed in life.

When it was time for me to go to middle school, I was so smart that they wanted to send me to a "gifted school." From what I can remember, it was a good school with a bunch of other kids who were just as smart as I was. If I went through it, I would have probably finished school early and all that.

This time, my mom agreed to it, and they set me up to take a test to see if I really had the brains to be there. If I went to that "special" school, I wouldn't be able to go to Cook Middle with my cousins and that wasn't happening. So what did I do? I went in to take the test and marked down anything. I didn't read it at all, just marked answers. The crazy thing was, after deliberately sabotaging my test I still only missed qualifying for the school by a couple of points. My mom was ticked! Maybe she was mad because she knew it was intentional, but I didn't care at all; I was going to Cook!

In my neighborhood during this era, the two biggest highlights of school life were going to Cook Middle and then Soldan High. They were the cool schools! Soldan had the best basketball team, football team, and band in the city, as far as high schools were concerned. Cook had a dope band too, but more than anything, coming from fifth grade, you couldn't wait to get to middle school with all the older, pretty girls. When we made it to Cook, most of the big homies were going to Soldan, so that gave us room to come in and take over. A couple of the big homies were still there, so that gave us leadership and back up. On my first day of middle school I was anxious, excited, nervous…all those feelings were going on at the same time. I was anxious to get there and see what it would be like. Excited because it was one of those life-defining, growing up moments, and nervous because I knew there would be a lot of pretty girls. I had to make sure my hair was right, kicks were on point, all that.

There were all kinds of people from elementary school and even people from around the hood, but the person waiting to meet Tank and me was Mr. Hudson. Mr. Hudson was the principal, and he had suspended a lot of my family members. Cook was right behind The Martanna, so all of my family went there, and they usually caused trouble, so my family's name rang bells with Mr. Hudson. "You two Billingsley's (even though that wasn't either of our last names), we're not going to have any trouble out of you two, okay?" Of course, we said what he wanted to hear, "Yes sir, Mr. Hudson," but we didn't know what we were going to do yet.

School was barely in and we were cliqued up with our own little gang: Woods, Tank, Corey, Lamont, and me; all we needed now was a name. After a bunch of corny name ideas we had it, "Jr. Rockers!" We already had respect because of our OGs, the ones still there and the ones who had just left. On top of that, Johnny's house was across the street from the school. On the days the big homies skipped school, they'd be on the porch or at the gate. It was always funny watching Mr. Hudson tell them to get away from the gate, talking to them like they still went there. They would talk crazy to Mr. Hudson and just walk off. Sweet Pea on the other hand, was another case. He was supposed to be there—he was skipping too—but he would never come to the gate, he would stay on the porch. Mr. Hudson knew when he didn't see our crew there, we were right across the street at Johnny's house, but there was nothing he could do about it. Mr. Hudson had this thing he used to do when he called you by your name. He would put a bunch of R's in front of your name like, "RRRRRRRRR-Travis, come here!" A lot of people have gotten in trouble just for laughing at that alone.

We were split up into different classes for homeroom and scattered in other rooms throughout the day, so lunchtime was where we gathered each day as a full team. It wasn't long before everybody knew that we were there to run the school—Mr. Hudson was the principal, but we were the law! In the authority line around there, you had Mr. Hudson and then us. Depending on who you asked, we had more authority with them than Mr. Hudson.

School hadn't been going for two months, and we had already started being wild. I would show up in the office and Woods would already be there. Tank would show up in the office, and I would already be there. Corey would come down, and Tank was already there. On top of that, we had a couple more dudes we ran with, now. We were doing all kinds of stuff around that school to all kinds of folks, but the last straw was when we jumped a new dude in the bathroom…at least, that's what he said. The truth was, we didn't jump him. He and another kid got into a fight, and a punch broke the new dude's jaw. He ratted us out to Mr. Hudson and told his parents that we jumped him…and not only that we jumped him, but also that we hit him with a gun and broke his jaw. The truth was, no one had a gun, but they didn't believe us. I guess they'd never heard of a person getting their jaw broken from a punch. That was it for us with the school; they'd had it with us!

That following week, they brought all of us into a classroom to have a meeting. When we got in the room, there were a couple of police officers, some teachers, Mr. Hudson, and this dude with an afro who was mean-mugging us as we walked in. Dude had on a suit that looked like it was from the 70s, and that fro wasn't helping him at all. He introduced himself, "Good morning, I am Mr. Washington, and I work for the St. Louis City Juvenile Denton Center." When he said that, no lie, my heart dropped! He went on to say, "I work with the gang division; we are here because your school is having a gang problem, and I hope to arrest somebody this morning." When Dude said that, my heart dropped even more—I didn't want to go to jail! I looked around the room, and everybody looked shaken. Once it settled in, that this dude didn't have anything on us, we were all cool. Another thing that became real plain at that point, we were a gang. By the end of the first semester, my grades were dropping, I had been to the office repeatedly, but at that time, I didn't care one bit. As long as I was with my family and in my hood, I didn't care about anything else.

Where I lived, it was rough. My neighborhood had three "project" complexes in it: The Cabanne Courts, The Alpha Village, and The Gardens. The west side as a whole had several hood gangs too: The B.O.D., The Horse Shoe, East Gate, Pershing, The West Posse (a.k.a. The Skan), Cates, and The Rockers (a.k.a. The Family). There were always plenty of people around to beef with, but apart from the occasional fights we usually got along. When Bloods and Crips came though, all of that changed fast. People you went to school with all your life, your childhood friends, and in some cases even your family, became your enemy.

The first time I heard about Crips and Bloods was from my homie Lamont. He came to school one day with a blue and black flannel shirt on, with just one button done at the top, a white t-shirt up under it, some blue Dickies pants, and some loc sunglasses. When I first saw him, I thought to myself, *This dude is a straight clown.* I even said to him, "Dog, you a fool, what in the world are you doing?" He looked at me with all seriousness and said, "I'm a Crip!" I said, "What?" He looked at me again and said, "I'm a Crip, Cuzz!" but this time, he took his hand and threw up a C sign with his fingers. I still had no clue what he was talking about, but I was convinced that whatever he was talking about, he was serious. So I asked him, "What is a Crip, and why are you wearing your shirt like that?" He said, "Crips are a gang from LA, and I'm in it now." I was even more confused, because we were obviously in St. Louis, and he was talking about being in a gang from LA. Before we left, he told me to go watch this movie called *Colors*, and I'd see what he was talking about.

That weekend, Tank and I watched *Colors*, and after it was over, I was a Crip too. I hadn't ever seen anything like it before. I had seen movies like *Rambo*, and others with killing, but they weren't like this. This made me want to be a gangster even more. I went back and watched that movie many more times, studying it, learning from it. I was going to be a Crip for real. I started wearing all blue. I know my momma was probably wondering what my new obsession was with blue, because it was all blue everything. I wasn't the only one who saw *Colors* and went crazy; you saw the effects all over the city. Everywhere you went, gang colors and tags were popping up on walls.

Right after *Colors* hit the city, we were flooded with gang members—real gang members from L.A.—that moved into different parts of the city and taught us the ways of "gang culture" for real. Their whole mission wasn't just to come show us how to bang. Their main mission was to come and make money, and they brought something with them that not only changed St. Louis forever, but also every city around America...crack.

Crack is the hard form of cocaine. Cocaine comes from a leaf called coca that's grown in Columbia. It's processed into a powder form and then shipped to the U.S. on boats and planes. Every person I know who's ever smoked crack says you'll never get that first high again no matter how much you smoke, so that's what keeps them wanting more and more. They call it "chasing the ghost," because what you are looking for isn't there. That summer, crack and gangs hit hard, and it tore the city apart. I don't think anyone was prepared for what either one brought to the city. It was like somebody released two monsters on St. Louis at once, not just St. Louis but every hood around America!

That crack was no joke. You saw grown women having sex with kids for it, teenagers smoked out, and people with nice homes, cars, and good jobs broke after a few months. But the money it made for the dealers was like nothing you'd ever seen! When crack first hit, people didn't see the damage it could do right away, so people were just trying it as if it were weed, but people learned fast that crack and weed are two different things. You could make three- to five-grand a day selling rocks, depending on where you were and the type of pack you had. I watched people go from heroes to zeros and zeros to heroes overnight, messing with that dope. Gangs were just as destructive, but an entirely different beast. Once the hoods made the decisions and picked sets—Bloods over here, Crips over there—it was on!

It seemed like everybody started getting money. In class, 12-year-old kids could be sitting there with two- or three-grand in their pockets! The first time I ever saw and learned about crack was at school while I was in the sixth grade. Dude in my class came to school with a bag of rocks and pulled them out to show me. We sat in the back of the classroom, and he gave me a crash course on Crack 101. The way people were going crazy over this stuff I thought that when he pulled it out of the bag, it would be glowing. It wasn't though; there was nothing fancy about the look at all, just a bag of little white pieces. Once he explained to me what they were worth, I saw a gold mine. He told me that each one of them was worth $20, and that he had $500-worth of them in the bag. I was like, "I can make five hundred dollars off of that?" "Easy," he said. He told me that people would pay twenty dollars for it, so they could smoke it in a pipe, and that if they didn't have money for it, they would sell their stuff and even rent out their cars. It was so hard to believe, but the stack of money he pulled out his pocket made me take him a little more seriously.

The second time I saw crack, I wasn't at school...it was at my house. There was this dude who used to come to my house every Friday night around the same time; the routine was the same, too. He would ring the doorbell, come in the house, walk to the kitchen with my momma and her boyfriend, and then leave right after. This dude came over so much that I wanted to see what they were doing in that kitchen. One night when he rang the bell, I timed it; I waited until they were headed to the door and rushed to the kitchen. When I walked in, I looked on the counter and saw a small plate with some rocks on it. It wasn't anywhere near what my dude had in class, but it was more than one. I dipped back out of the kitchen before they knew I was in there and went back to my room. I thought *Dang, that's tight, Momma sells rocks. We're about to have all kinds of money.* Inside, I knew that wasn't true, but I wanted to convince myself that it was. I was willing to believe anything at that point, as long as it didn't have to do with her smoking it.

No matter what I wanted to convince myself of, time would quickly replace my self-deception with the truth. That truth was, my momma wasn't selling rocks, but she was smoking them. It grew more and more obvious after a while; things got crazy fast. When I first found out my momma was getting high, we were living in our own nice apartment, momma worked hard, and we always had food and pretty much everything we wanted. It wasn't long before we started struggling. Momma couldn't buy us all the stuff we used to get. We tried to understand, but we started not having food sometimes, and then were behind on bills; it got bad quickly. Before long, we were moving out to live with somebody else.

The place we ended up moving to was my neighborhood's equivalent to The Carter, known as The Village. The Village, or should I say The Alpha Village, was a five-building project that was drug central. There were 100-plus apartments, most of the tenants got high, outside you had easily at least thirty dudes trapping all day, and nonstop traffic in and out of the parking lot, 24 hours a day. Crack was doing some people well, but the only thing crack got me was crammed in a side room on the third floor, in The Village, with my momma, my little brother, and her boyfriend.

CHAPTER 4
NEW JACK
SUMMER

My aunt's house was one of the main trap houses in the building. At any given time of the day, dudes were cooking, chopping, and bagging dope in the kitchen and were smoking it all over the house. My momma did her best to shelter my little brother from it as much as she could…she kept him locked in her room all day long. No matter how much she always wanted to protect us, that drug was just too much for her to protect us from. My refuge from the house was found outside—the same place that held all the trouble in the world I could get in to. Everybody around me was getting money. Kids in my same grade were coming to school driving cars, wearing fresh gear and jewelry, but I was suffering. I needed a way to get in the game, so I went outside to find one.

I didn't have an easy shot at getting my hands on some work (drugs). My family was highly respected in our neighborhood, so people wouldn't be so fast to put me on. I was frustrated and mad, but I didn't stop looking until I found somebody who would get me some work. His name was Blue. Blue was from The Garden's end of the projects, and funny thing was, he was only thirteen but had formed his own little crew. I was kicking it in the park one day and saw this kid from my school named Little Kevin; he told me that he was headed to the Chinese place down the street to have a meeting with Blue about getting some work and asked me to come. I knew Blue just from seeing him around the hood, but I never knew him to be a gangster or a hustler. He did dress like one, talk like one, but I never knew him to be one. We walked into the Chinamen, and there was Blue, sitting with three other dudes. I had seen the other guys before, but the only one that I recognized and knew by name was Primo. He was from The Gardens, too.

All eyes were definitely on me as I walked in, because everyone knew I wasn't supposed to be there. I quickly stated my case and let him know that Little Kevin had told me what was up and I wanted in. After a couple minutes of dialog, it was official. I was in. I didn't know enough about selling dope to contest the logistics of it. So, when he started talking splits, how much money we would get and how many rocks we would get, I just took it in as truth. We finished the meeting, agreeing to meet that Friday to pick up the rocks. I had seen the type of stash my big homies would have, I had seen other dudes flash work in class, so I'm thinking Blue was going to come with a nice pack. But what did he pull out that Friday? Five rocks! I looked at him like, *Cuzz, you calling a meeting to sell five rocks?* I couldn't believe it, but I was there now, so I thought *forget it*. We talked for a minute, and then he split them up. Primo got two, Little Kevin got two, and I got one. I couldn't believe this dude had called me down there for one rock, *one rock*.

I knew why he gave me one, though. He knew if I decided to keep whatever he gave me, there was nothing he could do about it. I took my one and ran with it, literally, straight down to The Village. I went out front and thought about my momma coming out and catching me, so I went further down, to Bartmer. Bartmer was already occupied, so I went to Maple, by The Martanna, where my people were. I saw one of the big homies that we called, "Two Eleven." After a couple minutes of small talk, I just flat-out asked him, "Big cuzz, how do you sell dope?" He looked at me like, "Little Travis, boy, your people are going to kill you if they catch you out here selling them rocks." I looked him in the eye and said, "I already do," and I flashed my stone at him. He laughed at me, "That's not dope, that's a little pebble. You're lucky to get $15 for it." Once he saw I was already about to jump head first in those streets, he gave me some game. After our talk, I knew what I could get for what prices, what I should make, and how to make certain moves. He even took my little stone and sold it for me.

I took that $20, gave Blue his cut, pocketed mine, and he gave me another stone. Before I got too far down the block, I sold the other one and was right back at Blue's again. He couldn't believe I came back that fast, but of course he was happy I came back at all. That time when I returned, he didn't have anything for me, so he took the two stones from Little Kevin and gave them to me, because Kevin was just standing around with them in his pocket. I got rid of those two, and we were done for the night.

Walking in our hallway at night, I was bound to see people doing anything. I'd seen people getting robbed, beat up, hustling, and even turning tricks. That walk from the first floor to the third floor in our building seemed like it took all day, only to get in the house and see the same thing. I couldn't wait to get back at it the next day.

By the time I caught up with Blue the next day, it was about three or four, and he still hadn't re-upped his supply. So, about five of us walked to The Village, over to his people's crib, so we could pick it up ourselves. We all sat in the living room while he went in a back room and bagged the work up. When Blue returned, he was cheesing hard. We were like, "Bruh, what are you smiling for?" He said, "Go look in the back room." We all jumped up and went to the back room, not knowing what to expect. There was a lady in there sitting on the bed. I was confused; all of us were confused. "Bruh, it's a lady, what's all the smiling for?" Blue said, "She's waiting on one of y'all to come in there," and then he pulled out some condoms. I had never used a condom before. I knew what they were from seeing them lying around and from people talking about them at school. None of my attempts at sex had ever worked, and here Blue was offering us all a shot at the goal. Blue had one of his cousins with us, some tall, skinny, goofy-looking dude named Larry. He jumped up fast like, "For real, she's down for that? I'm in!" He grabbed one of the condoms from Blue and went in the room.

I sat there with all types of thoughts rushing through my head. I was thinking so fast, it was like my head was spinning. I had wanted to have sex for so long, but as I said, I hadn't ever succeeded. Here was my opportunity. When the door opened up, Blue's cousin came out of the room with the same smile on his face that Blue had. We all looked around at each other, Primo looked at me, Little Kevin looked at him, I looked at Blue, he looked back at me, I looked back at the room, then I jumped up and took the one of the condoms. When I walked in that room, my heart was beating so fast – we're talking pounding-out-of-my-chest beating – but the smile she gave me helped take it down a little. I couldn't believe how nervous I was. Maybe I needed my uncle outside the door cheering me on, or maybe it was because this was a grown woman. Whatever it was, I got over it quick and then I left my virginity in that room with a woman more than twice my age. As I walked home that night, I couldn't believe what had happened to me over those past two days...the first couple of days of summer vacation. My run with Blue and his crew only lasted about another week; he couldn't keep the re-up going. The rest of my summer played out almost like a normal twelve-year-old's would, minus a few adult episodes.

That summer, so much had changed in the city, and the first school day reflected it all. Dudes that came to school bummy the year before walked in there looking like they had signed a record deal. A couple of dudes even drove cars to school. That may be normal for some high school students, but in middle school, not so much. And the girls... the girls had gotten prettier. Hands down, though, the biggest difference was the gangs. Over the summer, dudes had sided up and picked sets (gangs), so now you had dudes that you went to school with all your life, that lived just a few blocks away, who wanted to kill you or you them.

It wasn't just in school; it was in the hood, too. Gangs and crack took off like a rocket. The only thing going on was making money and killing, that's it. Freely crossing into certain neighborhoods got tighter and tighter by the week. If you weren't from there, you did not go, and even in your own neighborhood you'd better not be caught out wearing the wrong thing or you were dead. The first one of my boys to get killed was Leo. The news spread around the hood so fast, people kept saying over and over again, "Leo just got killed, and they found him in a gangway on Etzel." Everybody was crushed, especially Fox, because he and Leo were like brothers. I couldn't look at that gangway for a long time without it hurting. This was the first time I had dealt with death without it being an older person, and it wasn't a cool feeling. *What do we do now?* That's what I thought; that's probably what most of us thought.

Leo's funeral was the first hood funeral I ever went to, and it was sad. Have you ever seen a mother mourn over her only son, a sister crying over her big brother? It's not easy to watch. Neither is watching a grown man cry, a father weeping violently over his son's lifeless body, pleading with him, as if he could hear it and change the outcome. I was so hurt and confused. Those feelings quickly turned to something else, ANGER! That whole death thing was new, but that year we got familiar with it real fast...we had 177 murders in St. Louis and it didn't look like it would slow down any time soon.

My life was changing fast and it was starting to show up everywhere, even in my schoolwork. I got my first really bad report card ever that year. My momma couldn't believe it, but she knew some of the stuff I was doing, so she knew I was slipping before it happened. I didn't do anything in class. I would be there just to hang out with my boys, or I wouldn't be there at all because we were skipping. I would stay outside super late to keep from going to that hellhole of a house we lived in. I was changing, but the seasons weren't changing fast enough for me. I was looking forward to summer. I had big plans for getting out there and making money, but my momma saw all the trouble I was getting in to, and she had other plans.

I hadn't seen my daddy for about four years. I didn't even know how my momma got in touch with him, but somehow she did and arranged for me to live with him for the summer. To be honest, I was ticked off! I was happy to see my daddy, my little sister, and by then a little brother, but I wasn't looking forward to leaving. Living with my momma and little brother Shawn was all I knew, and I wanted to stay there to make sure they were all right.

My daddy no longer lived in Mississippi; he had moved to Detroit with my brother and sister's mom, Judy. I didn't know what to expect; I hadn't seen many places outside of St. Louis. After an 8-hour bus trip, my daddy picked me up at the Greyhound station. He still looked the same, but I assume I looked different to him. I was bigger—obviously, it was years later—my features had changed, and I had a little afro. Even though my daddy had let me down a lot of times before this, I was really happy to see him. It was also good to see my siblings. I hadn't seen my little sister since she was three; she was now almost nine. This was the first time I'd see my little one-year-old brother in person. When I got to my daddy's house, it seemed like they were doing pretty well for themselves. They didn't live in a mansion or anything, but they were doing way better than my current living situation. He and my stepmother both had cars, both worked jobs; rocked a little jewelry and nice clothes, and the kids had all kinds of stuff. On the other hand, I went to Detroit with next to nothing. Good thing for me that my stepmom loved shopping, so that changed real fast.

Once I settled in, I scouted the block to see what was going on. Before the end of the day, I found some dudes down the street that were just like me, hood. Dejuan and his little brother DeShawn were the first dudes I met on the block, and we cliqued up instantly. They had pit bulls, which I loved, and they had two sisters, Flossy and Daisha, who were both super cute. With every day that passed, I saw more and more that Detroit was just like St. Louis. It didn't matter how much this place was like home, I still missed my momma, brother, cousins, the hood, and especially my girlfriend Natasha.

My daddy worked for a charter school, so he was gone during the day. I never knew where my stepmom worked, but when she left, she dropped my brother and sister off at daycare. So, you know what that meant…I was left to myself, to do as I wanted for most of the summer. I spent a lot of time with Dejuan. Dejuan had a bunch of little brothers and sisters who stayed at their house, but he always talked about his big brother, Stony. The way Dejuan talked about Stony, he was a straight gangster, so it made perfect sense when I found out he was locked up. The stories made me want to meet him, but that would have to wait for another time.

You know how the saying goes: Time flies when you're having fun, and that it did. Summer was gone before I knew it. I had a ball up in there and managed to make it through the summer without getting into any real trouble. I also was able to spend a lot of time with my sister, brother, and daddy. I felt like my daddy and I were about to be on the right track, and that made me happier than ever. The last weekend I was there, my pop took me shopping so I could go home with some school clothes, and the whole family went to catch a movie.

My daddy didn't know it then, but he took me to see a movie that would have the same effect on me that *Colors* had, maybe even bigger. He took me to see one of the most gangster movies ever, made from an inner city point of view, *New Jack City*! I had never seen anything like this before in my life! I had seen gangster movies before, with those old Italian mob dudes, but I never felt like it was something within my reach. I mean, I wasn't old or Italian, so it didn't spark a flame in me like that. *Colors* made me want to bang, be a killer, and ride for my neighborhood but *New Jack City* made me want to get money, and get it by any means necessary. I rode that Greyhound back to St. Louis, thinking of a master plan. The whole ride, I was thinking about how to get money. I even thought about taking over The Martanna, but that wouldn't work. My granddaddy was the super, and the reality was, I didn't have the manpower to do anything like that anyway, at least not yet.

I came home to a surprise that summer's end. I expected to be going back to The Village to live, but to my surprise, Momma had gotten out of there. My momma is a beautiful woman, always has been. Even when she was getting high and losing all kinds of weight, she was still beautiful. When I saw Momma for the first time after getting home, she had gained all the weight back and was dressed up, like she used to be. While I had been gone, Momma got a new boyfriend and stopped getting high. She and my brother had already moved in with a dude named Tony. I had seen him around the hood, but I didn't really know him. All I knew was that I was happy he had stepped in, because just that fact alone had changed my life. No more being bunched up in that one little small room in that Village apartment. No more worrying about what we were going to eat that day. No more worrying that somebody was going to do something to my brother or momma there.

When we got to the house, he introduced himself. "What's up? I'm Tony." I answered, "I'm Travis," and that was that. It was so new for me, because I didn't know the dude, so I didn't know what kind of mission he would be on. He could be a psycho and end up beating on my momma or something, and for that reason, I didn't trust the dude yet. My new residence was on the south side, on Folsom, one street over from Blaine and two from McRee, two of the worst streets in the city.

CHAPTER 5
WHITE CHUNKS
IN A PLASTIC BAG

Even though we now lived on the south side, Momma kept me enrolled in Cook Middle, and I couldn't wait to get back. I hadn't seen my boys all summer, and eighth grade was about to be epic! Mr. Hudson made it known from the jump that he wasn't playing with us that year, and he was ready to prove it. School hadn't been in session for even two weeks before I was suspended for three days. When I got back from that suspension, I got suspended again for ten days.

He wasn't just suspending me; he suspended Tank, Woods, and everybody I ran with. Every time I got called into his office, I would hope that the jazz music he had been playing and my persuasive explanations would get me out of it, but no good. I think he was trying to hurry up and push me out. Needless to say, my momma was ticked. Shortly after my return from that suspension, like two days after, the bottom fell completely out.

It was second hour. I was in Mrs. Drips' class, doing what I normally did, clowning with my friends, and this girl named Nicole felt the need to say something about all of our playing. I said something back to her like, "Shut up!" She said something back. I said, "Keep talking, I'm going to slap you." She kept talking, and…I slapped her. I didn't straight slap her, like I would have slapped a dude, but I did tap her jaw a little. I wasn't about to full-out fight a girl, so I just kept walking away. I felt bad after it was over, because she was cool people, but at that moment I wasn't thinking. As soon as the commotion was over, Mrs. Drips sent both of us straight to the office, and Mr. Hudson was not pleased to see me at all. He just kept looking at me crazy the whole time Nicole told her side of the story. I was convinced before I walked in that office that no matter how the story was told, I would be the guilty party, but all of the attention was temporarily taken off me. That girl was so ticked at me that she went off on Mr. Hudson too…so bad that she got suspended! Once she was gone, it was my turn. I can't front, I was super nervous. He sat there behind that old desk, bobbing his head to the jazz song of the day while he filled out some papers. I knew I was about to get in trouble. I knew I would at least get sent home or even suspended for another three or ten. I also knew that Mr. Hudson was tired of all my friends and me, but I didn't think he was about to get gangster with it. He looked at me and said, "Mr. Tyler, you have been suspended from Cook Middle School for ninety days. At the end of your ninety days, you will have a hearing with the Board of Education to determine whether or not you can return here."

My jaw dropped! Who does that? How could you suspend somebody for ninety days? Was that even legal? Could I fight this in court? What in the world was this? My momma was going to kill me! I just got back in school, and here I was, suspended again, but this time for ninety days! I did not want to stay home for ninety days. School could be super boring at times, but being at home while everybody was at school would be even more boring. Lucky for me, I have the type of mom that doesn't just take whatever people hand out. She called the Board of Education and had a meeting scheduled for the next week. When we went before the board, my momma pled my case to them about how smart I was, how I had been around the wrong people, so on and so forth. Her plea at the hearing ended with her asking them to let me return to school, but not Cook. She pleaded with them to let me go to a different school so I could get a new start around some new people. They fired some questions back at Momma and then aimed some at me. I guess my mom's plea worked, because after a short time of deliberation, they gave me another chance. Even though I was happy about being able to go back to school, I had mixed emotions about it. I was all for going back to school, but I didn't want to go in another hood.

Monday morning, Momma and Tony took me to my new school, Grant Middle. I couldn't believe that I was so far out of my zone. Grant was so different from Cook, all the way down to how the classes were scheduled. First day there, I looked for somebody in there I knew, but it was just a bunch of unfamiliar faces everywhere I looked. One of them stood out, though, this cute little skinny girl name Candace. She was the friendliest person in the class, too; we cliqued instantly.

When classes switched, I saw a couple of people I knew from around my way, one of them being Little Kevin. I hadn't seen him since we were both trying to hustle with Blue. He had moved to the south side over the summer and had already made some ties at Grant, so he took me around and introduced me to some people. The most noticeable difference between Grant Middle and Cook were all the different ethnic groups. At Cook, the whole school was nothing but black people;

I think I saw one white person there the whole time. At Grant, there were black people, Asians, Hispanics, Bosnians, Africans, etc. Looking around the classroom, the last person I thought I would be cool with was the first person I cliqued up with, a white dude name Roderick. Roderick was the first white dude I ever kicked it with, but dude was cool as a fan.

My momma's boyfriend turned out to be cooler than I thought. He was straight looking out for us, big time. Outside of all of the material stuff he did for us, like shopping and feeding us, he really tried to be a father figure for me. There were a couple of other guys around who influenced me, too. Tony had a homeboy named Rich that was already living with him before we moved in. Rich was a straight player. He would sit and talk to me for hours about life, everything from women to money to cars. It was like Daniel-son and Mr. Miyagi; I soaked up everything he showed me. Also, an OG Crip named Big Sicc occupied the third apartment in our building; dude was banged out! My momma hated it when I talked to him, but Sicc put me up on a lot of game. He said he was from LA, but everybody at that point said they were from LA.

Sicc was like a gang historian; he knew everything about gangs, not just Crips, but Bloods, too. After hanging around Sicc I knew so much gang lingo, you would have thought I was from LA. I thought I was super-Crip. It was obvious that Sicc was trapping (selling drugs). He had people in and out of that place all day, but he wasn't selling to crack heads. I even saw Bloods going over there. One day I asked him, "What's up with that, how are you selling work to Bloods?" and his answer was, "Blood money spend too." He said, "You got to keep your enemies close, Cuzz." I understood that; it made sense and I knew the big homie knew what he was doing. Sicc had me come into his house one day and showed me around his crib. This dude was living like a king! His crib was plush, but what really caught my attention was the biggest gun I had seen in my life. "What's that, Sicc?" "That's an Uzi, little cuzz. You ever seen one of those?" "Naw, I have never seen one of those."

Sicc walked to the hall closet and pulled out a book bag. He walked back to the living room with the bag and had me sit down. He reached in the bag and pulled out a white chunk in a plastic bag. He said, "You ever saw some of this?" I lied and said "No," but I knew what it was all day. It was coke, cocaine, coca leaf, whatever you wanted to call it. I had seen it plenty of times, but never that much of it at one time before. Sicc starting handing it to me and said, "Here little cuzz, go and come up." I reached for it and he pulled it back. "Man, your momma would be beating my door down trying to kill me if I gave you this." What he said was one hundred percent true. We both laughed as he put the work away.

After school one day, I saw police cars and police everywhere around the block. I ran to my house, hoping my folks were cool. When I got to the front, I was relieved that it wasn't my house, but definitely didn't want to see the homie Sicc in the back of a detective car. I had seen police before, and those people weren't regular police. They didn't have on the regular city blues, they had on bulletproof vests, and they didn't have the regular handguns, they had machine guns. One of the dudes had a jacket on it that said "ATF," a couple of them had ski masks on…they were not playing.

I don't know what this dude Sicc had done, but they came to get him by any means necessary. I walked past the car they had him in, and I thought he'd be crying or something, but he wasn't. He just looked up at me, smiled, and winked.

I knew it would be a matter of time before the vultures started coming out, trying to get their hands on what the police didn't find in Sicc's house. As soon as the coast was clear, I made my way next door to Sicc's apartment to do my own search and seizure. Sicc had a stash spot that I knew the police wouldn't find. They could have torn that place down and still wouldn't find it. I went to the hall closet where Sicc kept this can; well, at least it looked like a can, but it was actually a stash spot. I could tell there was something in it by how heavy it was, and I had a pretty good idea what it was!

I made my way out of the back window, over the kitchen area, and into my room, a.k.a. the basement. I pulled out the can and unscrewed it, the same way I saw Sicc do, and there it was—white chunks in a plastic bag. I didn't know how much it was worth, but I knew one thing by the way it numbed my tongue... it was dope. I took some out of the bag and put it in another small bag, so I could take it to school with me the next day. I stashed the rest in our basement where I knew no one would find it.

I thought I had found crack in Sicc's apartment, because it was hard and white, but when I went to school the next day, I found out it wasn't. It was cocaine. Malcolm, the kid who told me it was raw when I showed it to him...his face lit up like a Christmas tree. I was hoping he had some money to buy it, but he didn't. So, we did the next best thing—I fronted it to him. I knew how much to sell rocks to smokers for, but I didn't know how to sell dope wholesale. I just said the first thing came to mind, "Give me forty dollars." I knew I had beaten myself, because he looked too happy and took it too fast.

That evening I was at home and my momma told me somebody was at the door for me. That kid Malcolm was at the door with twenty dollars and a mouth full of rocks. He came to show me that he got it rocked up, and that he was already out there selling. He also wanted to make sure I had some more work, which I did, but I didn't need him knocking on my door too many more times. We had to come up with a system, some kind of way I could serve him and not have him knocking on my door twenty times a day. Maybe he could call and let me know when he was low, but then he would be calling too much. Maybe I could get a pager, but then my mom would wonder why I had a pager. Man, I didn't know how to keep this thing going. I didn't have to rack my brain too hard or long, Malcolm made it easy for me. He didn't pay, so I cut him off fast, problem solved. Well, at least that problem was solved, but I still had another problem. I had work that needed to be sold. I decided to go to the hood Friday when I got out of school.

Friday couldn't come fast enough. I almost jumped off of the school bus before it stopped rolling. I ran into the house, said, "what's up" to Momma, and ran straight to the basement to my stash. I still had no clue of what I had, how much it was worth, or how to cook it up. I grabbed another plastic bag and split the stash in half, so I could take it to the hood with me. I grabbed a bike that was in our basement and went upstairs to say "bye" to Momma, but she was gone. I wrote her a note: *Momma, I rode a bike to the west side, I will call you later from Grandma Bee's house,* and I dipped.

When I made it to the hood, the first person I saw was a smoker named Chubby. Everybody knew Chubby, and I knew he would know how to help me get this done. In normal circumstances, it wouldn't be a good idea to let a smoker cook up your work, but Chubby hadn't always been a smoker. When I was a little kid, he was a hustler. I guess somewhere down the line he decided to sample his own product. Since then, he'd been out there chasing that ghost. I guess nobody ever told him rule number one, as Sicc told me—"Don't get high off your own supply." It was sad to see, especially since he used to be out there getting money. Chubby knew my momma, my aunties, he knew how young I was, but when I told him I had that work, he was more than ready to help me out. We went to this trap house, an almost vacant-looking trap house that he used to be in with another old dude named Mr. James. We went in a side room, I pulled out the coke, and his eyes got big. He didn't think I'd pull out a stash like that. The room already had all the tools we needed to make this happen. It was obvious they had cooked dope in there before, and maybe a lot of it. Chubby didn't offer as much coaching as Sicc did, all he was concerned about was getting something to get high. I broke him off some of the finished product, took my pack, and dipped out.

I thought after I got the work cooked, my problems were over, but I didn't think about what could be a bigger problem—selling the stuff. I had to be extra low key, because my momma didn't know I was out there trapping. I couldn't tell some of the big homies, because they would probably take it from me and send my butt home. I had to do this thing on the low, for real, so I was thinking hard. Then it hit me. I was a kid on a bike...I could ride around moving product and nobody would think anything about it.

By kicking Chubby some extra work, I guaranteed that he would bring me as much business as possible. It didn't start out fast, but once it got going, it was popping. Before I knew it, it was almost midnight! Man, my granny would kill me, knocking on the door that time of night. I had to get to her house fast! I don't think I have ever been as nervous as I was knocking on my granny's door. Good thing for me she was asleep, because if she had been awake when I knocked, I would've had a problem. I just knew when she opened that door, she would know what I had been doing, but she didn't. She just fussed a little and let me in.

That weekend would become the template for every weekend after that. I would go to school all week on the south side, stunt with the little money I was making on the west, and then on the weekend it was back to the hood to get it in. My momma had no clue at that point what I was up to; even when I would buy some new stuff, it was cool, because my step pop was always buying me stuff. People at school used to assume what I was doing, because I would come to school with new stuff and showing money.

I lived for the weekends. I couldn't wait to get back to the block, not just so I could get on my grind, but so I could see my cousins. This was the first time I had lived away from them since we were little kids. Thunder was a couple years younger than Tank and I, but we were always around each other. Even though we were cousins, Tank and I were more like her big brothers. She had her momma and her little brother but they struggled just like we did. A lot of people think being on welfare is a privilege for the families receiving it, but it's not. You can't raise two kids, getting $250 to $400 a month. That's a story we all knew firsthand, but it didn't break us, it made us closer. It made us love each other harder. It made us survivors! Everything we had, we shared. Even with a quarter, we'd walk to the corner store and the person who had it shared with everybody, getting a 25-cent bag of cookies or something. If someone had two dollars and we were all hungry, we'd go to the Chinese spot and get a half-order of rice to split. If one of us ate, we all ate; if one didn't eat, we all didn't eat.

Gangs didn't slack in the city, and as more people got killed, I made a decision. It was time to get a gun. My plan was to buy one, but I knew I would have a hard time doing that in the hood without my family possibly knowing. I didn't want to buy one from just anybody on the street; it could already have a body on it. That's when it hit me... my step daddy had a gun at our house that was always kept in the same spot. He never moved it or went into the room where it was; he would never know it was gone, so I decided to take it. That was the first time I had held a gun. It was a 38-revolver, brown handle, lots of scratches on it, but it was pretty! I didn't know if I was nervous because I knew I could get caught with it in my room, or because I knew I had something in my hand that could end somebody else's life with one squeeze. Maybe it was both.

That weekend when I went to the hood, the first person I found was Tank, so he could see the gun. We both passed it back and forth, then the question came up, "You got bullets for it?" Not only did I have bullets for it, I had enough to load it two times. I had been practicing how to load and unload it. The only thing I hadn't tried yet was shooting it. We loaded the gun up, walked behind a vacant building on Maple, and found a spot where nobody would see us. My heart was beating fast. My hand was getting sweaty and I was nervous, but my hand wasn't shaking. I took the gun, cocked the hammer back, pointed it to the sky, and squeezed the trigger. BOW! Then I hit it again, BOW, BOW, BOW! I felt such a rush, from the kick back in my grip, the echo that rang out against the brick wall we were by, and the adrenaline flowing through me! I passed it to Tank, and he fired off the last two shots, "BOW, BOW."

I started carrying that thing everywhere I went, school included. South side was mostly all Bloods, and I considered myself a Crip. Little Kevin was on the same mission that I was, me on the west side and him on the south side, so I stayed connected with him. He sometimes acted flakey, and one day I'd had all I could take of him. We were in the schoolyard and he just was talking some ole crazy stuff that I wasn't even in the mood for. I told him to chill, but he wouldn't, he just kept talking reckless. I told him to shut up, but he didn't listen. Before I knew it, I had my hands around his neck, choking him out! While I was roughing him up, a bullet fell out of my pocket and hit the ground! Before I could pick it up, one of the kids who was watching us saw it. I knew from the look in his eye, he was going to tell. Sure enough, he did.

Later that day during class, an announcement went out over the loud speaker. "There will be a school-wide locker search before the end of the school day." WHAT? All the days with the gun at school, I'd had no problems at all, now one instance of messing with a dude and I'm caught. I had to think of something fast. I didn't know how far they were along with the search, so I didn't want to go to my locker and get the gun … if they were right there, man, I'd be stuck. I asked my teacher if I could use the bathroom. My plan was to leave, and it seemed like a good one until I went to the hallway where the principal saw me and called me to the office.

I wanted to turn around and get out of there, but I just kept my cool and went to the office. I just knew they had the gun in there, I just knew it. My heart was beating so fast; I thought I was about to have a heart attack. When I walked into the office and saw Little Kevin, I just knew he had ratted me out. As the principal started talking, I realized she had no clue about the gun. We were in there about our little altercation on the schoolyard. The principal gave us both a pep talk, we apologized, and she let us get out of there. In the hall, I asked Little Kevin why he didn't tell the principal on me. He apologized again and said; "That's in the past, let's get back to the money." Since he wanted to be cool, I thought, *Hey, why not put him right back to work?* I sent him to my locker to get the gun, and off he went.

When the school bell rang, the locker searches were done, the gun was out of the building, and I was a happy person! After school, Little Kevin met me by my bus. Even though I sent him to get the gun, I still didn't fully trust him, so I had him give it to Shauna. Shauna was a girl who lived two streets over from me, and we rode the same bus. I knew she liked me, but I never felt that way about her; I just kept her around for times like this. I kept thinking that the police were going to pull us over and take me off the bus and straight to jail, but they didn't. All of my anxiety was gone when we got to the bus stop. I was clear! I told Shauna to take the pistol to her house, and I would come get it later on. She was cool with that; she wanted me to come over there anyway. She had been trying to get me over to her house forever, but little did she know that I was coming to get my gun and leaving.

I walked through my front door, super happy that I didn't get caught. At least, that's what I thought. But, the first thing I heard was, "WHAT DID YOU DO THIS TIME!?" "What are you talking about, Momma?" Her question was so broad. I did so much stuff; she could be talking about anything. She said, "At school, what did you do at school to get suspended?"

I knew it wasn't the gun, because we got that out. The only other thing I could think of was the incident with Little Kevin, but the principal had said we were cool. I truly didn't know, but of course that was not the truth momma wanted; it just sounded like a lie.

The following Monday morning, we went to the school for a meeting with the principal and assistant principal, to find out what I had done. As we walked in, we saw Candace and KeKe, two of my friends, in the hall. They came to speak to my momma and looked at me like I was walking "the green mile." The principal didn't look excited to see me at all; I hadn't really given her any trouble, so I didn't understand it. We sat down; the principal greeted my momma and then turned right to me. "Do you know why you are suspended?" "No ma'am, I don't, I was hoping you would tell me." She said, "Friday we did a locker search, and we found something in your locker." I was confused. "You didn't find anything in my locker but books." She said, "No, actually, we found this..." She reached into her drawer, and pulled out a zip lock bag with a knife in it. I looked like *What?!* When I saw the knife, I instantly knew where it had come from. Earlier in the year, KeKe had put it in my locker, and it had been in there since. All I could think was, "I AM DONE!" I had gotten the gun out of the school but had forgotten there was a knife in my locker! The principal told me that they did the locker search because they heard I had a gun, but when they searched the lockers, they found the knife. She asked if it was mine, and I said, "No," because it wasn't. When they asked whose it was, though, I said I didn't know. So, of course, in their eyes, that made it mine, and that ensured my suspension.

I was officially suspended for the rest of the school year, with a hearing pending at the Board of Education to determine my full punishment. The principal told my mom if the knife would have been one inch longer, I would've gone to jail, because it would have been considered a deadly weapon.

I couldn't believe it. I had just come to Grant because I got kicked out of Cook, and now I was suspended for the rest of the year! KeKe was in the hall when we came out, and she could tell that whatever was wrong was bad. I told her I wasn't coming back the rest of the year. I didn't want to tell her why, because I knew what she was would try to do. When I did, she said exactly what I thought she would, "Tell them it's mine." I couldn't do that and wouldn't do that; I was trying to protect her. I had never heard of a person being suspended that long before. Three days—normal, ten days—you're in trouble, ninety days—you're wilding out, but the rest of the school year? That's unheard of. My only hope was the meeting with the school board.

I was hoping they would hear my story and let me come back to school, but that was far from what happened. When I went to the school board meeting, you would think I had stabbed and killed somebody with the knife, the way they were on me. I walked out of there hearing something I couldn't believe: "Travis Tyler, you are indefinitely suspended, and can never attend another St. Louis Public School as long as you live." When the superintendent told me that, I could have died, and the look my momma gave me should have killed me! I really felt like I was being sentenced to jail time. The only difference was that instead of being sent to Boonville State Prison, I was being sent to Tri-A. Tri-A was an alternative school for kids with behavior issues, a.k.a. "the bad kids."

In my opinion, that is one of the dumbest ideas in the world. You take all the kids from different neighborhoods, different gangs, boys and girls who love to fight, shoot, whatever, and put them in one school. I never could understand that idea; how could anyone think it would be healthy?

My momma definitely didn't think it was a good idea, so she came up with another one—sending me to live with my daddy. There were a few things wrong with that idea: One, even though I loved my daddy, we had no relationship. Two, Detroit was just as bad as St. Louis. Three, I didn't want to move there. It was one thing to go visit for the summer, but an entirely different thing to move there as my home. Even though my mom was doing a lot better, I still didn't want to leave her or my little brother. I didn't want to be gone from my cousins that long either. I couldn't believe that all of this had happened over a dumb kitchen knife that didn't look sharp enough to cut a bologna sandwich. I might as well have gotten caught with the gun! My mom didn't waste any time getting me out of there, either. She got in touch with my daddy, who, to my surprise, said yes to me coming. Momma put me on the first Greyhound smoking out of St. Louis.

CHAPTER 6
DON'T EVER
COME BACK

I hadn't seen my daddy since that past summer. A lot had changed for me since then, even the way I looked. I had grown in height, weight, and even attitude. I know my daddy probably had no clue that since the last time I saw him, I had a little Nino Brown in me. I was used to being out on the weekends, getting money, and I didn't know if my daddy would go for that. To my benefit, little had changed when I arrived. My daddy still worked every day, came home late, and Dejuan and DeShawn still lived on the block. That meant I would have plenty of room to get just about anything I wanted popping.

When I got there, school was already in session, so I came in with everything in motion. Dejuan and I were the same age, so we went to the same school. Detroit was supposed to be a new start for me, a different environment, new people, all that. But, Detroit was just like St. Louis, and I was quickly on the same mission up there. Our school was a distance from my daddy's house, so Dejuan and I had to catch the bus. Dejuan's grandma lived right by the school, so that made skipping easy. We skipped so many school days that I was surprised when I passed. But, I did, and as long as

I passed, I had no issues with my daddy. Even though I was now staying with him, I still felt the same way I did when I was with my mom, because between working and whatever else he was doing while he was gone, I didn't see him. I wasn't complaining though, because it left me plenty of time to get into action.

After spending a little bit of time with my daddy, it didn't take me long to figure out where I got my thing for the ladies from, because Daddy was a player. I imagine most folks talk to their daddies about cars, money, stocks, bonds, and things of that nature. Let's be realistic, where I'm from, you don't talk to your daddy about too much of anything because he's not there. Some folks where I'm from don't even know who their daddy is, so that's why I didn't care if we talked about girls or paper planes, I was just happy to be talking to him. Every now and then, Pops would try to drop a little nugget on me, but he talked to me like I was still a kid. In theory I was, but mentally I had already processed some of the experiences he would speak of hypothetically. He would try to school me on girls, but I had already been with women. He would talk to me about gangs, but I was already running with killers. My pops had no idea who he was feeding and giving shelter to; I was far from the little boy he whooped in Greenwood for busting a screen door.

The first time I was in Detroit, Dejuan's big brother, Stony, was in jail, but this time he was on his way home. From what Dejuan would say, Stony was a straight G and a hustler—my type of person. Dejuan liked doing dumb stuff or messing with dogs, but he wasn't about two things that I was about, which were girls and money. So, when Stony touched down that summer, I was looking forward to seeing if he really was all that Dejuan said he was.

Dejuan had a white red-nosed girl pit bull named Red. She didn't look like much at first, but once she got older, she was a beast. The only person in the neighborhood with a dog that looked better than Red was this OG named White Mike. When I first heard somebody say his name, I thought it was super funny, because he was as black as I am. But once I learned more about him, I knew why they called him that… because he had that "white," a.k.a. cocaine. White Mike had two nice puppy pits. Every time he walked them past my house, I would make small talk with him. Yeah, it was true, I did love dogs, but I wasn't trying to connect with him to get dog-breeding tips. I wanted in on the hustle.

When Stony was released and got back home, he was on the same mission I was on. Since the moment I saw *New Jack City*, I was on a "take over the world"-type mission, and I didn't care where it was—Detroit, St. Louis, Mississippi, wherever—it didn't matter. It didn't take long before I was hanging with Stony. When I got home from school every day, nobody was there to tell me what do. My stepmom, brother, and sister got home around five, depending on the day. My daddy got in most days super late, and by that time, I was either just getting back home myself, or I was still out. My stepmom looked out for me and showed me love, but I know it had to be a big change for her to have me in the house. I was a big teenager, and she knew the type of trouble I got into at home. My daddy didn't have to deal with me much, because he was there but he wasn't there, you know. We did stuff and kicked it, but on the day to day I was on my own.

For the most part, I stayed out of his way and we didn't have any problems, except for when I got bad grades. By this time, I was in ninth grade, and I was doing nothing in class—literally just sitting there, chilling—or skipping, walking around Detroit or over at somebody's house. My pops knew I could do the work and that I was playing games, but he didn't know I saw no need for school at that point in my life. What I wanted to be, I didn't need to go to school. What I wanted to be, I didn't need to sit through an hour of Home Economics or Typing every day.

I wanted to be a gangster. He should have understood, because he did too, when he was my age. My grandparents had to get him out of Chicago when he was my age, because he was running around with gangsters, getting shot at and all that, so he should have known more than anybody. That life had me out until three or four in the morning, in a city I wasn't from, trying to get money. That's when we started having real problems. Pops felt like I was disrespecting his house by coming in those hours.

Stony used to have us on some missions! I knew enough about the streets to know that if we were going to be on these missions, we needed a gun. I knew where I could get one. My daddy had a nice little 32 at the house and didn't seem to ever use it. It was easy getting a hold of it, because he hid it in plain sight and never really checked the box. The next time I went out with Stony, we were good. We had work and we had heat. The first couple of days I took it, I snuck it back into the room while my daddy was at work so I wouldn't get busted. After a few days, I got comfortable knowing that he wasn't checking it and started keeping it. I even took it to school with me.

Once White Mike saw me hanging with Stony, he spent more time talking to me, too. One night, I was on his porch, messing with the dogs, and the police drove down the block. I got shook and almost took off running before they even stopped. Mike noticed how I responded and knew something was up. "Little bro, what you get all spooked for? You acting like you got something on you."

"I do, I got that heat," and I showed him the pistol.

"Where you get that from, you out there putting in work?"

"If I have to, I will. I'm just trying to make sure I'm good out here, that's all."

"That's a nice little piece. You have to let me carry that sometime. All my guns are big; I could hide that easily." The next night, I let Mike use the pistol while he went to make a run. It took Mike forever to get back, and when he did, he didn't have the gun. He gave me the story that while he was out, the police swooped on him, so he stashed the pistol in the bushes and left. Supposedly he went back to get the pistol after they left but couldn't find it. I didn't know what to think or believe, but I knew one thing…I couldn't go home without that pistol. I told Mike the whole deal, that it was my daddy's gun and I couldn't go home without that gun, so we came up with a plan. I would stay at Mike's house, and he'd give me some money to catch the Greyhound back to St. Louis.

All I had to do was sneak back into the house while my daddy was at work, get my clothes, and bounce back to the Lou (St. Louis). My plan shouldn't have been that hard, but we all know how this type of stuff goes. When I didn't come home that night, the first thing my daddy did was look to see if his pistol was gone. He sat in the living room all night, waiting on me to come in, and when I didn't, he called off work and kept waiting.

About 10 a.m. I went to the house, thinking no one would be there. I coached myself all the way down the alley, "It's easy, in the house, get your clothes, back out the door, and on the Greyhound back to St. Louis. It's easy!" We stayed in a two-family flat, so I had one flight of stairs to go up. I took my key, opened the bottom lock, and eased in the door. When I got to our door, I went to stick my key in the door and saw the knob turning. I turned around and got out of Dodge! I ran down the steps, out of the front door, across the street, and headed to the alley! I made it halfway across the street, looked back, and saw my daddy running behind me with a belt in his hand. He ran a couple more steps and stopped, because he knew he wasn't going to catch me.

I ran like Forrest Gump! I didn't stop running until I thought I was in the clear. I couldn't run right back to Mike's house; it was too close. I didn't know if my dad had jumped in the car to look for me, or what, so I just ran. I walked around the city all day until it got dark. After walking around all day, I stopped at a pay phone and called my granny. I told her some of what happened, but didn't mention the gun. I told her I wanted to come home, but Granny told me I needed to stay in Detroit. I hadn't talked to Granny too long before somebody set a car on fire in the liquor store parking lot I was standing in, so I had to hang up and get out of there! I know my granny about freaked out, because all she heard was, "I've got to go, somebody just set this car on fire and it looks like it's about to blow up!" "This car" could have been the car I was in for all she knew. She didn't know if I was walking, running, or swimming, all she knew was that I had run away and was out in the street.

While we were on the phone, she gave me her brother's number, my Uncle Willie, and told me to call him because he lived in Detroit. When I got somewhere that I could use a pay phone again, I called Uncle Willie like my granny had said to do, and he had an earful for me. When he told me that my granny called him, all upset, I didn't want to hear that. I hated to see my granny upset over me. To her, I was still her grandbaby, and I wanted to keep it that way. My granny told my Uncle Willie to pick me up, take me to my daddy's house to get my clothes, and take me to the bus station, in that order.

I couldn't believe it; I'd be going back home! Something good came out of this mess, but first I had to go get my clothes and face my daddy. I had my uncle pick me up from White Mike's house, because I had left some things over there that I needed to get. I could tell Mike was happy I was getting out of there, but as I was leaving, he didn't offer me a thing—no money, no work, nothing. I went to the basement, grabbed my clothes, and on the way out I went to where I knew he stashed his work. Mike had taken my gun and thought he was about to play me. I found his stash, grabbed a bag and took about a quarter ounce. That should pay for my gun!

My uncle drove me to my daddy's house. When we knocked on the door, he already had my stuff ready. I walked in expecting something totally different than what happened. He asked, "Where's my gun?" I said, "I lost it." Then my daddy looked me in my eyes and said, "Get your stuff, get out my house, and don't come back. You are never welcome in my house again." I can't lie; I was crushed! I thought he would whoop me, yell at me, do something, and then tell me it's cool, we'll work it out, but instead he ex-communicated me, his son. I wanted to go back to St. Louis, but I didn't want to go back because my father had sent me away for good. Truthfully, I don't know why I didn't cry, because I was crushed. I went back to my Uncle Willie's house for the night, and the next day I was on a Greyhound, headed back to St. Louis.

CHAPTER 7
I CAN SEE THE ARCH

When I got back to St. Louis, everything was different. When I'd left, my momma was staying with her boyfriend, Tony, doing well. But when I got back, she was staying with my Auntie Shea again. The only thing that was different about this situation was that they weren't living in The Village anymore; they were staying on a street named Wells. Wells and Kingshighway was a Blood neighborhood. I knew that because they were cool with my neighborhood, and that was the only reason I could even come on that street with blue on, thinking I was a Crip.

When I made it back to the Lou, it was the weekend, and you know the first thing I did—I went straight to Maple. I missed my cousins. I couldn't wait to tell them all the stuff that I had done in Detroit and show them what I had come back with. I sat them down at the table, pulled out the dope, and said, "This is crack." Then I took it out of the bag, set it on the table, and said, "This how you cut it up. This is worth ten, this is worth twenty, and this is worth fifty. As long as you remember that, you will never be hungry or broke."

When I left St. Louis, I knew about hustling, but add what I knew then to what I learned in Detroit, and it was on.

I took Thunder with me around the corner so I could start selling the work. I had always told Thunder that I'd look out for her, that I would get money, and we wouldn't go through the struggle forever. I was determined to keep my promise to her. We left Martanna walking and cut through the lots, headed over by The Gardens and The Village. Before we could get to Bartmer, we saw a bunch of police. Thunder was young, just turned 11, and there was no way the police would bother her, so she took the work. She took the pack and stuck it in her shoe, and we cut on through the hood.

We went straight through the hood and down by The Gardens so Thunder could holler at one of her friends. We weren't there thirty minutes, before Thunder and her friend got into it with some new girls that had just moved in. I was sitting back, just watching and making sure everything stayed even, then I remembered something—Thunder had the pack! By the time I thought about it, Thunder had her shoe off, beating a girl with it, and there went the pack. We looked all over the yard, but we could not find that work. I wasn't even mad, though; it was my little cuzz, and she didn't mean to do it. I just had to find another way to get my hands on some more.

There was no one to tell me what to do. My momma had slipped further down, and I hadn't talked to my daddy since leaving Detroit...I was pretty much on my own. I would leave home and be gone for days. Nobody cared. I would be out all night hustling or just out with my people. I would spend the night on Maple most nights, and sleep at Thunder's house in a back room. Thunder and I would sit up for hours, listening to the radio and talking about how we were going to get out of there.

A lot had changed when I got back from Detroit. My little cousin Dudda was obviously following in my footsteps. He had his own little crew and everything. It was Dudda, Wayne, and Little Joe; they were even driving. Little Joe was a car thief. Every time you saw him, he had a stolo (stolen car). Dudda had learned to drive, and he was only twelve. Seeing this, I knew I had to learn how to drive. There's no way my little 12-year-old cousin was driving and I wasn't.

One night, Joe came back with a car and showed me how to drive. It didn't take me long to figure it out, and once I did, I was rolling. I drove around all night!! We had that car stashed for about a week. We would park it during the day and hop back in it after dark. The person whose car it was must have been into church, because there were Bibles in the car and even a green glass cross hanging from the rearview mirror. One day, I hopped in the car to go driving and forgot my screwdriver to start it up, so I looked all around that car for something to start it with. I looked at the cross, then took it down from around that mirror and used it to start the car up.

Once I was done with that car, I graduated fast from stolen cars. It just wasn't my thing. If you got caught in a stolo, you were going to juvie (Juvenile Hall). So instead of stealing cars, I rented them from crack heads. That way I didn't have to worry about going to jail, I would just get dropped off at home if the police caught me. I had smokers who would rent me their car all week, and the smokers who worked all week would rent me their car all weekend. I really loved the weekend ones, because they would spend their whole check with you before they started renting out their car. One of my favorite customers was a white boy named Ron. Ron showed up every weekend like clockwork. When he came over, I would take him over to this lady named Kandy's house, in The Gardens. He would stay there all weekend, getting high. Saturday nights, while he was sitting there getting high, we would take his car and go to a skating rink called Saints. While everybody else was getting dropped off and picked up by a ride, I was driving myself, at the age of fourteen.

Kandy used to be all in. She'd have let Ron stay there for a whole month, as long as he had that dope. I would sit in the house and just wait for him to come out of the room. It was like sitting at an ATM. There was something that kept me in Kandy's house more than getting money on the weekend. Kandy had a daughter named Monica, and that was my dawg! The first time I saw Monica, I was posted on the steps by her house, hustling, and she was walking from her school bus. She always had a good girl, I-don't-belong-over-here type of look on the outside, but she was from the hood, just like us. Maybe it was the little Catholic schoolgirl-looking outfit she had to wear to school that made it look that way, I don't know, but she just didn't look like she belonged there. Monica and I instantly cliqued, because we had so much in common. I thought at first she would hate me when she found out I used to serve her momma that work, but she didn't. Kandy would try to fake, calling me to her room like she wanted something else, but I knew that Monica knew what I was doing.

Before long, our buddy-buddy relationship turned into something totally different. I went from staying over there late on the weekend to me spending the night. Kandy didn't care what I did in that house as long as I kept fuel in her spaceship. Hustling was quickly becoming a full time job for me, and school was interfering with my grind. So, I started taking more and more days off from school. I didn't have a problem not going to Tri-A anyway, it was super boring. I'd rather sleep at home than sit in there any day. As soon as school was out, whether I went or not, I went straight to the block.

I used to be the only dude in the midst of the whole hood who claimed to be Crip. That is, until the day my big homie Q talked to me. I was sitting on the steps, posted in The Gardens, and Q walked up and was like "Travis, you tripping, blood. You're running around here all day with this blue on and those fools are out here killing our homies. You have to stop all that. We're family, you tripping." I sat there for a minute and thought, *You know what, he's right.* No questions asked, I decided he was right and started banging for the hood hard. Before Big Q and I talked, I would already ride for the hood, but after our talk I turned up even more. I instantly started rocking red everything. Red belt, hoodie, cardinal fitted, whatever, it didn't matter, I just wanted it to be known I was from my zone.

If it weren't for my Granny Bee, a lot of days we would have gone hungry. Every week she faithfully brought boxes of groceries. If you didn't know my granny, you would think she was balling and owned some kind of company or something, but she didn't. She was a maid for a rich white family. You couldn't tell, because she dressed nicely, always had money, a car, and her house was laid! When I was younger, whenever the family she worked for went out of town, she would take me over there with her to watch their house. They lived in Clayton. Clayton is the part of the city that you drive around to look at the big houses and marvel at how dope they are...the type of houses you look at and wonder what jobs the people who live in them must have. That's Clayton. The funny thing is, Clayton was so close to the hood that we could touch it, but it still seemed so far away. For the people in this particular house, the husband was a doctor and the wife was a lawyer. My granny would tell me that I could be a doctor or a lawyer when I grew up, too.

She believed that, and she was right. I was smart enough to be either one, but something happened somewhere between those conversations we'd have, to me standing in a bathroom with a mouth full of pills. There I was, standing in the bathroom with a mouth full of pills, asking myself over and over again, *What am I doing?* I was hurt, and the truth was, I didn't want to die but I wanted everybody to know that life was hurting me so badly that it made me want to die! I wanted my daddy to hear about it, call me, and say he loved me and that I was welcome back at his house. I wanted my momma to know how bad I was hurting and stop getting high. But in the end, all I got was a ride to the hospital, a cup of charcoal, vomit on my shirt, and a few days of observation. My granny still had hopes that I could turn it around. She asked me to stay with her.

My granny didn't have a clue what type of person I was growing up to be; all she knew was the little boy who used to ride with her to flea markets and K-mart on the weekends. The little boy who would lay on her living room floor for hours, listening to music on her stereo while eating all of her snacks. She quickly found out that I wasn't that same kid, because every chance I got I was skipping school, staying out past my curfew, or getting caught sneaking some girl into the house. A part of me wanted to do right, because I loved my granny. She was one of the few people in the world that I even cared what they thought of me, but I felt like it was too late. I was so used to doing everything for myself, that the things she was doing for me weren't enough in my mind. There I was, going to a school where all the kids rocked hundred-dollar kicks (shoes) with expensive clothes, and there was Granny, buying me Goodwill clothes. I hated disrespecting my granny, so I would try to be in on time, but on the weekends and even on school days, that was super whack. Granny was patient with me, though. I'd knock at all times of night. I just knew that she would kill me when she unlocked those bars, but she'd just let me in. Well, I wouldn't say she did nothing—she did fuss at me. When I would walk past her at night, on her knees praying, I knew that she was praying for me.

My momma and auntie never lived anywhere too long, so it didn't shock me when they had to move again. This time they moved into The Martanna. This left me with a situation on my hands: on one hand, I could stay with my granny and deal with all the rules but have a clean house to live in and food to eat, or I could go back to my momma's house with all kinds of freedom. For me, the choice was easy, I moved back in with my mom. I didn't care what the situation was; I had to get back out, because Granny had me on lockdown. The cost of my freedom from Granny's rules didn't come cheap. The situation we moved to on Maple was definitely crazy. We had people in and out, just like we did in The Village, especially on the weekends. Money would go out as fast as it came in, and because there were so many people who lived in the house, food would go just as fast. It got rough. The worst night I can remember happened that winter. It was freezing cold and our gas was cut off. My auntie, her kids, and her boyfriend were all piled up in her room with a space heater. My momma and brother slept in a small room with a space heater, and I was in the living room balled up on the couch in a sleeping bag. I vividly remember how cold it was that night. I had to use the bathroom so badly, but I didn't want to get up. I lay there all night, hungry and cold, hoping it would be morning soon. The sun coming up meant a couple of things to me: one, it would be warm so I could get out of the sleeping bag, and two, I could go to school and eat.

I didn't understand life, but I understood that I had to make the best of it. Often when life was crazy, I just needed to get out of that house. I used to find peace just a few feet away from my front door, at the second-floor hallway window. I would stand at that window and imagine taking flight. I would fly away from all the craziness around me without my feet ever leaving the ground. I would think about all kinds of stuff. I would imagine living in Clayton. I would wonder what it would be like to not have to worry about what I would eat or not having heat in the winter.

One day as I stood there looking out that window, watching life happening, words just flowed from my mouth: "How am I going to get out of here?" And something inside spoke and said, "MUSIC." Music? Music was like my doorway to Narnia. Since I was a kid, I found some sort of peace in it. Whether it was me lying on my granny's floor listening to it, me in my house at night with all the lights off zoning out to it, or Thunder and I sitting up all night talking while it played in the background. Music was always there for me.

The Martanna was a big building, and the basement had two sides. My granddaddy turned one side into an apartment and the other side was a storage space with a boiler room. My Uncle James had a whole bunch of stuff in the storage room that had been down there for years. As kids we used to go through there running and playing when we were little, but had never really paid attention to what was down there. One day I decided to look through some of the stuff and found some things I definitely could use. Hidden behind a pile of junk I found two big house speakers, an amp receiver, and matching tape deck. I dusted it all off and took it upstairs to my room so I could see if it worked. Those speakers looked like they would knock...they had a twelve-inch sub and tweeters in them. I found wire to hook everything up, cut it on, and yes they did knock!

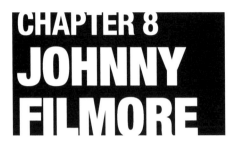

CHAPTER 8
JOHNNY
FILMORE

When we moved on Maple, I went to school when I felt like it. It wasn't like anybody cared; I just had to stay out of the way of the truancy officers. Drugs took over the hood so fast, I don't think anybody was ready for it. So much dope was being moved that the dudes with dope had to find somebody to sell it, and dudes like me were prime candidates. Everybody knew my situation. They knew the mission my mom was on, they knew the type of stuff that was popping off in our house, and everybody was trying to recruit me to be on their team. Out of all the offers I got, the homie Black Rich made the best one. I already looked up to him because he was really getting money! So when he called me to the side and dropped that work on me, I didn't even need to think about it.

I had a problem, though. Even though there was all traffic coming through my house, my momma still didn't know I was hustling. It wasn't long before one of the smokers ratted me out, and the cat was out the bag. I was really into it by then—I had a little safe, a revolver, and I had started making and stacking a couple dollars. One particular day I had decided to go to school and when I made it back home, I got the surprise of my life. Somebody had broken the lock off of my safe and taken everything out of it! Momma was the first person I called, even though I didn't think she took it. But after I was ready to wild out on my aunt's boyfriend, my mom admitted she had done it. I learned from that mistake and knew I couldn't stash anything in the house while I was gone, or even while I was there.

When I started selling my momma drugs, our whole mother-son dynamic changed completely. I don't know if it was because she felt like she didn't have any more authority with me because I knew she got high or what, but I pretty much was grown from that point. I went to school when I felt like it, came home when I wanted to, supported myself, all of that. I was on my own.

I loved the hood life and everything about it. The dudes from my neighborhood weren't some random group of people that I had started hanging with; they were my family. We'd been together since we were pups. We had been broke together, hungry together, all that! We started calling ourselves The Family, because that's what we were—family. We loved each other, but the downside to that was just like any other family, we hurt together, too.

Johnny Filmore—to me, Johnny was everything I wanted to be. It wasn't because he was rich, because he wasn't, or because he had a bunch of cars or women; it was because he was a soldier, a leader who would fight for his people and lead them with no fear. Johnny had a white Buick Ninety-Eight. It was like a 1982 or so, old school four-door, nothing too fancy. The white paint wasn't fresh and the burgundy interior was just decent for a car that old, but the trunk! He had some beats in that thing! We always knew when Johnny was coming, because we'd hear him beating all the way down the block. Most of the homies had beats in their ride but you always knew when it was Johnny, because he was playing the same song all day long—Tupac, *Violent*. "They claim that I'm violent, just 'cause I refuse to be silent, these hypocrites are having fits cause I'm not buying it!" The beat was a simple but hypnotic baseline that went over and over again, but it sounded so crazy on a Kenwood and some subs. There wasn't a day that went by that I didn't hear that beat going past me, either walking through the hood, standing in front of The Martanna, or while I was sitting in the house.

I spent the night over at my auntie's house one weekend, and I saw that car in my dreams. The whole time while I was asleep, I saw Johnny's car just riding, beating *Violent*. In my dream there was no sky, city, streets, nothing at all. It was like a black backdrop, the kind like you take pictures in front of. The only other thing in the dream was Johnny's Ninety-Eight, riding and beating hard! It just kept going and going and going, like in real life, but then it started slowing down, and I noticed somebody calling my name. "Travis, Travis! Wake up!" The music stopped as my eyes opened to see my auntie standing over me, handing me her phone. It was my momma. Barely awake, I heard my momma say, "I'm calling to tell you that your friend Johnny's dead. Somebody killed him around the corner." Johnny's white Ninety-Eight had just turned ghost. That was the last time I would see him ride. I was crushed. I could not believe it. That dude was a giant to me, unbreakable, and now he was dead. I wanted to go home right then. I needed to know what happened. I needed to be with my brothers. I knew the whole hood would be crushed; they all loved him like I did, some more. I needed to get to my people. I hoped that it was all some sick dream that I was having, but it wasn't.

Johnny's funeral had Hoods in it from all over the city. He was a general and all the soldiers and other generals came out to pay their respect to our "Fallen King." I will never forget the pain that Miss Filmore had on her face, sitting on that front row, the way his son, Little Johnny's, momma cried, or the hurt that the hardest homies had on their faces sitting on those funeral home benches. I was holding back my tears and wiping the ones that were escaping through my eyes as I sat there, with this hurt and anger growing on the inside of me. I wanted to just bawl uncontrollably. My heart was in need of some kind of answers, but there was no one around who could answer me. They all looked just as crushed as I felt.

This wasn't the first time I had felt like this. They say death comes in threes, right? Well, this was the third time, two of them in less than a year. Leo was killed first; he was only sixteen. They found him dead by the side of a building. Second was Gus. Whoever killed him dumped his body on the east side and he was found months later. Third, Johnny— he was murdered in the hood. I couldn't believe that I'd never see the big homie riding around the hood again. "Johnny, I never got a chance to thank you, Big Bruh, for taking up for me when that big dude was bullying me and for showing me that I didn't have to be afraid. For being the big brother I never had, for always being there." That's what I wanted to say as I stood in front of his casket on my turn to view the body. I stood there for a while. This wasn't Johnny. I was so used to seeing Johnny up on his feet, taller than most people at 6'3, talking loud, laughing hard; that was the Johnny I knew. This wasn't Johnny; this was just a shell. I pulled a tape out of my pocket and clutched it in my hand, a tape that I had recorded *Violent* on, back to back, on both sides, so it would keep flipping and playing nonstop. I figured if Johnny were going to be riding like he was in my dream, he would need that song. I stuck the tape in the pocket of his red and black flannel shirt, and then walked out, confused, hurt and angry.

When Johnny died, most of the people who lived through that would say that The Family died with him, and I would agree. What came after that was worse. Boom, Boom, Boom! That's all you heard, every day and all night! Then you would watch the news the next day and see nothing but bodies dropping. St. Louis had turned into "Gangland." We were banging in the Midwest like we were in Compton or something.

It seemed like the more "gangster" the hood became, the more "gangster" the music became too. I remember being a young boy and hearing the type of music my momma would listen to. It had a groove, made you want to chill. The stuff we had now made you want to ride, and by ride I'm not referring to driving a car. It was hip-hop, and I loved it. Whenever I was home, I was locked in the back room with my music banging as loud as it could go. The first time I heard *The Hood Took Me Under*, I felt like this dude MC Eiht (eight) was speaking to me, for me, and about me. When I first heard Scarface on N 2 Deep, I went crazy! But the first time I heard *Pocket Full of Stones*, by UGK, I found the sound track to my life.

CHAPTER 9
FOURTEEN

It was crazy, the effect crack was having on the world. That crack would make a grown woman have sex with a kid, a grown man rent a car that costs thousands of dollars for a $20 rock, and that's not the worst people were doing out there. Even my mom…I watched that work bring her down to her lowest point, and just when it looked like it couldn't get any worse, it did. I saw the police swoop down on our building, and the first thing I thought was, they're about to kick in my door. I watched from the porch across the street as the police went into my house and came back out with all of the kids. I could hear my auntie, the kids, and even my momma crying from across the street. It was chaotic. I saw the police take all of the kids out except for my little brother. As soon as those police pulled away, I hurried to the house. My auntie's boyfriend was walking back and forth, mad, and my auntie was crying like crazy. My momma was crying and putting on clothes. "I have to go get my baby and make sure he's okay." When the police knocked on the front door, my momma had my little brother run out of the back door to my granny's house. The police who came to my house weren't just looking for drugs. They were with people from the state, and they came to take all of the kids. When they checked our house, it was just like they suspected—so they did what they came to do.

The next day, their job was complete when my mom turned my brother and me in to the social worker at the juvenile court. I didn't know where those people were taking us, how far away it was, or how long we would have to stay. I knew my momma loved us no matter what she did. She sacrificed for us all my life; that went without saying. But, my momma LOVED my little brother, sometimes I felt like more than me, even though I knew that wasn't true. Before we were taken, my momma told my little brother, "I'm coming to get you, I promise!" With her voice cracking and her eyes full of tears, I saw the sacrifice and strength that Momma has always shown peep out for a minute. I knew she would come. She did what the state told her she needed to do, and she got us back, but not before we spent some time in the system.

Due to the difference in our ages, they had to split my little brother and me up. He went to a group home behind the juvie center, and I went to a place called Y.E.S. in University City. I didn't have a clue where they had taken my little cousins; I just hoped they weren't as uncomfortable as I was. I was used to being around family, and lots of family, and now here I was, dropped off by the social worker at a group home.

I didn't know what to expect. From the outside you would think it was just a four-family flat, but it was far from that. The first floor apartments were an office, storage space, sitting area, and kitchen. The upstairs apartments were converted into a computer room, a sitting area, a boys' side, and a girls' side. Where we slept, there were like eight beds in a huge room, almost like a prison dorm. I hadn't ever been in this type of situation before. I lay there all night, the room dimly lit from the moon shining through the window. All I could think about was my momma and my little brother. How was she holding up? Was he somewhere scared? My little cousins; where were my little cousins? I know it had to be scary for them, because they were little kids. Truthfully, it was a little scary for me, but I wasn't going to show that.

The room there may have looked like a jail, but it wasn't jail by a long shot. The kids were far from criminals. We had video games, snacks with every meal, and there were girls. If they had thrown the rules out of the window, it would have almost felt like a vacation spot. All of the amenities made it a little easy to settle in. I was still worried about my mom and brother, but this place was a cakewalk. They even let me leave campus for school. After a couple days in, my caseworker showed up to take me to get a physical so I could start school. The first thing she said to me when I got in the car was, "I hope you're in the mood for some crying. I have to pick up a little girl to go with us. She's been crying since the day she was placed." I was definitely not in the mood to hear any crying, but what choice did I have in the situation?

When we pulled up to what she called a "temporary foster home," she went in and came back out with, as promised, "a crying little girl." As they got closer to the car, I realized I had heard that crying before. That "crying little girl" was my little cousin, Tiffany; she was taken with us the other day. As soon as she saw me, she stopped crying and came to me. I was so hurt and so happy at the same time, to know the little girl that had been crying for days was my family. I held her the whole ride, all the way to the doctor and back. When it was time for us to take her back, I didn't want to let her go. The second we pulled back up to the house where we picked her up from, she knew what was about to happen and she started crying again. I was crushed because I couldn't help her...I couldn't even help myself.

My dreams of going back home with my momma didn't come true at first. The state approved my granddaddy to take me to his house, and for whatever unknown amount of time it would be my new home. You'd think this would make me happy, being out of the group home and with family, but I wasn't. I love my granddaddy, but his house wasn't my house, and I wanted to go home. Granddaddy had a little house pushed back far off the street. As small as the house looked on the outside, on the inside it was pretty big. There was a living room, a garage, kitchen, and two bedrooms. Granddaddy had one of the rooms all set up when I got there, with a bed and a dresser. I was all uptight about going there at first, but once I got there and saw how life would be set up, I loosened up some. My granddaddy worked construction, so he was out of the house early every day. Most nights he came in beat and he was out for the count, snoring fast. Granddaddy gave me a lot a freedom, but I didn't want to jump out there too wild too fast, so I paced myself. I walked straight home from school every day and chilled. I had my own little room; it had a bed, a telephone, a TV, I was good. Once I had worked my way into the system and earned some trust, I asked if I could go out on the weekend, and he said I could. Even though he gave me the whole "don't be down there hanging out in that neighborhood" speech, he knew where I was going.

When I moved in with Granddaddy, the state started sending my $50 monthly child support check there. Granddaddy wasn't hurting for money, so he would cash it and give it to me. What Granddaddy didn't know was, when

I got that money, I went straight to the hood every weekend and hustled as much as I could. As long as I stuck to the rules, we had no problems; but once Granddaddy let me get too comfortable, I got loose. I started having my homeboy pick me up from school every day instead of just on the weekend, and some nights I stayed out super late. I used to go out on the weekend and come home every night, but now I would go out on the weekend and stay gone until Sunday night. It's wasn't long before Granddaddy started to get fed up with my mess. I think he honestly may have wanted to send me back, but before he could get a chance, my momma finished her program.

When the state took us, they gave my momma certain requirements she had to meet in order to get us back. She had to complete a treatment program and provide a stable living environment for us. She did everything the state required her to do and then some. While she was in treatment, not only did she stay clean, she also got a job, and as soon as they released her, an apartment. When the state took us kids, a group of our family members stepped up and had us live with them until our mommas got it together. My little brother and one of my cousins went to stay with my aunt, the two youngest with my uncle and his wife, my granny took the two oldest, and of course, I went with my granddaddy. As happy a day as this should have been for my brother and me, I couldn't fully rejoice. My momma looked beautiful when she came home. She was a totally different person than she used to be...this was the momma I knew from growing up. You would think this would be a fairytale moment and an amazing reunion that led to happy endings and endless family moments, but it wasn't. You see, my Momma had been rehabilitated, but I hadn't.

I thought I could do all the stuff I was doing before we left. Momma was cool with it then, so I thought she'd be cool with it now. I didn't waste any time trying to find out what I would be able to do. I started staying out all times of the night and continued slacking in school. It wasn't long before I stopped coming home or going to school all together. The only time I saw home was when my momma was at work, and I went in to get clothes to change and wash. I had pretty much moved in with Monica. I had clothes there, I went there every night, and we slept in the same bed together. I think it's safe for me to say I lived there.

At fourteen years old, every idea you have is a good idea. You spend very little time thinking about consequences, because you think you're smarter than everyone that has ever lived. Every plan ends well in your mind, because today you're winning and tomorrow would be even better. A knock on Kandy's front door at six o'clock in the morning was not abnormal. When I heard the knock, I immediately thought it was a smoker, but the voice on the other side of the door woke me up faster than Folgers. "Police, open up!" I went back to Kandy's room and told her to go to the door to see what's up. She went to the door and got the same response as I did, "Police! Open up!" This time they added a little more. "We're looking for Travis Tyler. Is he in there?" When I heard that, my heart dropped and I went into survival mode. I didn't know what the police wanted with me, and with all the stuff I had done, I was not trying to find out. Kandy had steel bars on her front door, so I knew they couldn't get in until someone let them in. That gave me time to think while we were stalling them out. I ran back to Monica's room, grabbed my gun and my work with plans to jump out of the window and run, but there was a policeman standing out back to make sure that didn't happen. There was only one other way out of there, and that was the front door.

Okay, let me calm down! What am I going to do? I'm trapped! Let me think. Okay, I can flush the dope and hide the pistol. If they find it, I'll claim it, and if they don't, I'm good. I was sick to my stomach, flushing that work down the toilet, but I would rather take a loss and have my freedom. Kandy was giving me plenty of time. She was walking around, acting like she was looking for the key to unlock the door; the whole time the key was on her key ring. Once I had flushed the blow, I took the pistol, shoved it in the dirty clothes hamper, and came out of the bathroom. Kandy opened the front door and the police officers walked in, looked at all of us, and asked, "Is Travis Tyler in here?" When he asked that, it became obvious that he didn't know what I looked like, and before I could even get it out of my mouth, Kandy said what I was thinking. "No, he's not here." I couldn't believe it! It didn't matter what they wanted with me, they didn't even know who I was. Before I could get too happy about the situation, I heard a familiar voice say, "That's him, that's Travis right there," and that voice belonged to my momma.

I couldn't believe it. At least now I knew what it was about. Momma had called them on me because I hadn't been home since God only knew when. She didn't just come with the law; she came with the caseworker, too. That was it for me, game over! The police walked over to me, cuffed me up, and led me out of the door. Kandy and Monica were both crying. I didn't know what was about to happen or where they were about to take me. I knew it wouldn't be jail, because I was only fourteen, but I also knew that they didn't go through all of this trouble to take me home.

They put me in the police car and we tailed my caseworker to my momma's house. Once there, an officer helped me out of the police car, took the handcuffs off, and my caseworker gave me instructions. "We are going in here so you can take a shower, pack your clothes, and then we are going take a ride." Take a ride where? I was so ticked at my momma that I didn't even say "bye" when I left. I just gave her a look like; "I can't believe you're doing this to me." She looked at me and said, "I got help, now it's your turn."

I'm going to get help? What in the world do I need help for? Are they taking me to a rehab or something? What's going on? Based on the direction we were headed, it looked I was going back to Y.E.S., but then I remembered...the caseworker told me that if I ever ran from that group home, she would send me somewhere that was stricter. I think running from home got me in the same boat. Once we rode through the city and hit the highway, I knew it was all bad. We rode 55-South for about an hour before I finally asked where we were going. Even though my question was answered, I had no idea where Flat River, Missouri was. Finally, we pulled into a small town that seemed like something out of Andy Griffith. We drove through the town, onto a single road; then we followed that for a few minutes before pulling up to a flat ranch-style house.

"Travis, are you awake?"

"Yes I'm awake, where are we?"

"This is your new home for a while. Grab your things and let's go inside."

This is crazy man! I'm out here in the middle of nowhere, for God only knows how long. This is not cool at all. I didn't know what kind of place it was; I just hoped it was halfway as cool as Y.E.S. The first thing we came to was an information desk with two people behind it. It was strange, because it looked like a living room with a TV, couch, chairs...you know, living room stuff, but then here was this information desk, like at a hospital. There were doors on both sides of the wall behind the desk, and as we got closer, you could see that one led to a kitchen or something. There were two long hallways that went down both sides of the building, and both hallways had doors lined up on both sides, around twelve doors on each side. It was obvious they were expecting me, because they already knew my name. "Hi, you must be Travis. We're glad you had a safe trip." They told me I could sit at the TV while my caseworker took care of the business and signed me in.

It must have been close to school letting out when we got there, because shortly after I sat down, kids started coming in. This could be a strange place to live, based on the type of people coming in. There wasn't a common theme at all. After a parade of all different kinds of folks coming through that door, the only one to say something to me was the last one to come in, a girl named Ladonna. She walked over, introduced herself and shot a little game at me. "What you looking all mad for?"

"What should I be doing, smiling like you? You should be mad that these folks got you locked up out here in the woods."

"Locked up? We're not locked up; there aren't any bars on these windows or doors. We're misplaced, but not locked up. When I first came, I was mad just like you, but being mad isn't going to get me out of here. Anyway, what's your name and where are you from?" We exchanged names and found out we were both from St. Louis. When my social worker was done, she said her goodbyes and left me in the care of the staff. She pretty much left me in limbo. I had to wait until she called back to tell me how long I would even be there. I was ticked off, to say the least. Here I was, in the middle of nowhere, fell asleep on the highway so I didn't really even know where I was, and on top of that, didn't know how long I'd be there. The staff knew I was mad, and I'm sure the caseworker had filled them in on the type of stuff they thought I was into at home.

They checked me in and searched me to make sure I didn't have anything on me that was dangerous or illegal. After the search, they gave me a tour of the facility and told me the rules. They showed me the kitchen, the dining area, and the laundry room, along with showing the chore list of what each person did. Then they gave me the rules about the girls' side and the boys' side. The information desk and the living room were the middle grounds; boys were not allowed on the girls' side and girls were not allowed on the boys' side. The girls' side had the staff office and the isolation room, and trust me, that isolation room didn't look like a place you wanted to visit. Once they gave me the rules and showed me around, they took me to my room. The room had a bed, chair, desk, a closet, and space for a TV or something. I had to remember that this was not a good thing, because for a minute I got happy.

After I was there a couple days, I got a call with the verdict on how long I would be there—four years! The social worker told me that she and my momma decided that I needed to stay there until I was 18. I couldn't believe it, but there was nothing I could do about it. The way I saw it was, I had two choices. One, find a way out of there, or two, make myself at home. I decided to make myself at home until I found a way to get out of there. The house staff made it pretty easy to get used to the place. They were all cool in different ways. When I told them I liked music, they found me an old radio in the storage room that a kid had left behind. While we were in the storage room, I saw some hand weights that I wanted and they let me get those, too.

We had a house full of kids there, but I only dealt with a few. The main two were Ladonna and a kid named Gerald, who was also from St. Louis. The more we three talked, the more we found that we had experienced a lot of the same things and even knew some of the same people. Talking about the city with them was one of my favorite pastimes, but it also made me homesick. There was another kid there from St. Louis named Dre, but I hadn't met him yet, because when I arrived he was with his family for a funeral. The staff had already given me the heads-up that he might not like Ladonna being all in my face, seeing that she and he were supposed to be boyfriend-girlfriend.

It was hard sleeping in that place. A couple of times, I woke up in the middle of the night after dreaming that I was at home. Those dreams seemed so real; I just knew I was about to wake up in a familiar bed. It was like those dreams you have about money where you wake up gripping your hand like money is there; they were that real. The more days went by, my communication with everybody at home got further away. I used to get a letter and sometimes a call from Monica at first, but now, nothing. I hadn't received one call from my daddy yet, and the calls from my momma were even getting scarce.

Every day, I thought about the fact that I was stuck in that home until I was 18, and every day I thought about running away from there. I asked the other kids how successful people had been running away, and they told me lots of people had run. Sometimes they would get away and stay gone for a long time, and other times they'd get caught and be brought right back. Ladonna had tried a couple of times, and both times they brought her right back. I knew not to ask her for help. After being there for a few weeks something started happening that I wasn't expecting, I actually started liking it. In spite of the fact that I hated being away from my hood and my family, there was a certain thing I liked about being at this group home. I didn't have to worry about how I was going to eat, because they fed us good. I didn't have to worry about the gas or anything else getting cut off. I didn't have to worry about any beef either, because there were no gangs there.

One of the things that helped me cope besides the weights and the radio was writing. I would mainly write stories, until one day one of the staff people gave me an idea. "Why don't you write your own raps? You rap those songs you listen to real good." I had thought about it before, but had never sat down and tried it. I didn't even know where to start, so after sitting there forever trying to decide, I just started writing. "I'm in a place that I don't want to be / walls closing in on me," once I got the first line, the rest started flowing like water. Before I knew it, I had a whole page, and then I turned it over to fill up the back. I had no clue what I was doing, all I knew was, it felt good to be writing and getting the stuff out that I felt. I vented about everything I was going through. I talked about Johnny getting killed, my daddy, how I felt about being in that place, everything. When I was finished, I sat there looking at the paper, thinking how it was full of my inner thoughts. It was like I was writing in a diary, writing stuff that I didn't normally say out loud. So that's what I called it: "The Diary of a Mad Man." When I finished, I said it for the staff member who had suggested that I write, and he loved it (minus the fact that I cussed several times).

No matter how cool that place was or seemed to be, there was nothing cool about being there on the holidays. Thanksgiving is one of those holidays that if you have family you get together with them. Even if the people in your family don't get along, Thanksgiving is one of those times everybody comes together anyway. That year, while my family was together for the holiday, I was sitting around a table with people I had grown to like, but they weren't my family. They tried to make it feel like home; we had decorations and everything else that we would have at home. We carved pumpkins for Halloween, stuffed turkeys for Thanksgiving, and of course decorated a tree for Christmas, but it still wasn't home. The thought of Christmas approaching only made Thanksgiving more painful for me. The group home tried their best to make it comfortable for us, but no matter what they did, it was hard. It was even harder watching kids get to go home for the holiday.

It's amazing how the human brain is so creative and powerful that it can imagine a scenario in your head that you believe can come true. I'd lay in my bed those nights leading up to Christmas and dream with my eyes open. In my dream, I was surprised by my family with gifts and smiles. My daddy was even there, and he was going back home with us! After all those years of wishing, my dreams would come true; on Christmas morning I would see them play out in real time.

The scenario was well-rehearsed by the time Christmas morning came, because I had lived it out in my head so many times. The way it played out in real time was so dramatically different, that I wished I could have gone into a dream state and just lived it in my head instead of waking up that morning. As I woke up and climbed out of bed, I could hear a mix of Christmas music and laughter coming from the day room. I put on a t-shirt, threw on my house shoes, and made my way towards the celebration with my heart full of joy! I watched the kids excited and laughing as they ripped through the gifts they got from the group home or gifts their family had sent, waiting for my turn. When it was my turn, I opened the gifts that the group home gave me, not bothered by the fact that none were from my family, because I knew what would happen; they were going to bring my gifts with them. I sat around all day, waiting for my family to come walking through those doors. But hopes of that happening faded with every second of the setting sun. This was not how it was supposed to end. The day was supposed to end with us riding back to St. Louis together as a family; but instead it was just me, in a group home, on Christmas.

With every sunrise and sunset, my patience got thinner. I was supposed be there for four years, and I didn't know how I'd just gotten through the past four minutes. The room was starting to feel smaller, the bed was starting to feel uncomfortable, and living in that house with those kids every day was getting to me. I was at my breaking point, so I needed an escape plan. Since Ladonna had tried to run away from there more than once but got caught every time, she was off my list of advisors. St. Louis was too far away to walk and it was winter, so walking was out of the question. I wasn't one to be hitchhiking either, jumping into a car with some random stranger who could be a serial killer. The only thing that made sense was for me to drive. The fact that I was in the woods with no car should have put the brakes on my escape plan, but when the kid in a room next to you is a car thief, there is a way!

As soon as I hit the TV room the next day, I approached Little Gerald to have a pow-wow. In less than five minutes, Little Gerald was convinced to steal a car. He had one stipulation…he had to come with me. Another person involved increased the chance of me getting caught, but on the other hand, it would be at least a two-hour drive and I could use somebody to ride with me.

After our little meeting we had an official plan. We would steal one of the staff workers' cars and drive back to St. Louis. I can't lie, even though I wanted my freedom, the situation was kind of hard. Each one of the staff members was super nice to me, so there was no easy way to pick whose car we would steal. I was the mastermind behind the great escape, but Gerald ended up making the car decision. If you know anything about stealing cars, the way you start the car is through the steering column, so the ones with nothing around the steering column are the easiest to get. So, the decision actually made itself; we had to steal the car that was easiest to break down.

We had the staff routine down to a science. Bedtime was nine o'clock, and then the staff checked the rooms every fifteen minutes. You could hear the doors opening and closing as they moved down the hall. The biggest gap of time we'd have would be when the overnight staff came at eleven o'clock and they had to switch shifts. The plan was that after eleven o'clock check, Gerald would climb out of the window, break the car down, and then climb back inside until the next check. We would already be dressed in bed, with our bags packed, so that after the 11:15 check we could both head out of the window and be gone before 11:30.

Eleven o'clock came. I heard Gerald's window open. Five minutes later, I heard it close, and then I heard the tap on the wall to let me know he was done. This was it...after the next check we'd be out the window and on our way back to St. Louis! That's what I thought, but when I heard the door open to Gerald's room a couple of minutes early and heard the staff tell him to get up, I knew something was wrong. I jumped out of bed, took my clothes off, dumped my packed bag into the closet, and lay back down like I'd been asleep the whole time. A few minutes later they started doing room checks and came straight to mine since I was next door to Gerald. I just lay there, pretending to be asleep. When they opened up the door, I acted as if the light woke me up. They made me stand up, as they did everyone else, to see what I had on, making sure I didn't have clothes on under my covers. They checked my skin to see if I was cold and checked my closet to see where my clothes were. When they were done, all I got was, "Clean up your closet tomorrow, it's a mess."

Once the chaos calmed down a little bit, I got up to ask if I could get some water, but really I wanted to see where Gerald was and how he was holding up. When I walked near the front desk, I saw him. They had him in this little library room and that boy looked shook! I just walked past and gave him that look like "Don't rat me out, bruh" and kept moving, because I didn't want them to think anything of it. I lingered at the water fountain long enough to hear the overnight staff say what alerted him. He said he went outside to smoke a cigarette, and while he was outside he heard something making noise around the side of the building. When he walked around the building, he found what was making the noise—Gerald's plastic bag blowing in the wind. I told Gerald not to put anything outside until we were ready to go, but obviously he didn't listen and got caught. Our whole plan was messed up now that he'd gotten caught. They were going to have their eyes on all of us now. I knew I should have tried an escape by myself!

Things turned up to a whole other level when the staff person tried to start her car and leave. She came back in asking for help, confused as to what was going on. "I keep turning my key, but it won't make a sound or start." After several attempts of trying to start her car, she found out what Gerald and I already knew…it was broke down. When the staff found out that the car was broke down, the level of trouble Gerald was in went up 100 notches. I just knew he was going to rat me out when they started talking about jail, but he didn't; he just rode it out.

Security around the place went up to a level four, code orange, after that night. Every time you looked around, staff was there. It made it hard for me to have my run-ins with Ladonna; there was no sneaking at all. I was already frustrated and ready to get out of the home before, but after our failed escape I really hated being there. I'd had few problems since I had been there and the staff loved me because I was chill, but my frustration and anxiousness to leave quickly turned into other issues. Every day we had chores, and when we didn't do them we had consequences. At this point I really didn't care so my chores became a problem, and when I didn't do them I got the consequences.

I woke up one certain morning in a bad mood, and a kid named Rob, who tended to act racist towards me, kept calling me "boy." After what I considered being a fair amount of warnings, let's just say Rob ended up face down on the floor. I had him locked up, smashing his face into the carpet, and didn't plan on stopping until he stopped calling me, "boy." He pretty much had his mind made up that he wasn't going stop, and I had my mind made up that I was going to keep him locked up and continue smashing his face into the carpet. By the time the staff got me off of him, he was looking like a red crayon.

The staff saw me as the aggressor, which I was, so they restrained me. I made it easy for them; my issue wasn't with them, so I didn't take it out on them, I just complied. My heart sank when I found out they were taking me to the isolation room. There was no way I deserved to go in there, but because my issue wasn't with them, I did what they said. The isolation room was 8 feet x 10 feet, with no furniture, bed, or chairs; it had nothing at all. The carpet in there was thin, all four walls were metal, the door was solid wood, and it had a small window with a metal gate-like thing over it. When I first walked in there I thought I would be cool, but when that door shut, all of a sudden that room felt way too small. My mind knew that I couldn't get out of there, so I did the first thing that I knew to do in my panic—I started kicking the door as hard as I could! That door didn't budge, no matter how hard I kicked. "Let me out of here!" I yelled, I kicked, they wouldn't listen, and so I kicked harder. After a while, I felt dizzy. The room just kept closing in on me, so I lay down on the floor and looked under the crack in the hallway until I calmed down. I hated the way I was feeling right then; I wasn't in control. They could leave me in that room the rest of my life and there wasn't a thing I could do about it. I just wanted to be free, but that wasn't happening.

I thought I was dreaming when I heard her voice. "Baby, you need to calm down, you got them scared out here. If you want to get out of there, you need to stay calm." One of the staff let Ladonna come to the door to talk to me, hoping she could talk me into calming down. I didn't want to be calm, I wanted out, but it looked like one was the price for the other. They kept me in that room all evening; they wouldn't even let me out to use the bathroom while the other kids were still awake. I sat in that room, second by second, pacing back and forth. I was about to lose it again. The only thing that kept me calm was when I started rapping. I had memorized the songs I'd written, said other people's songs, and even came up with new ideas. While I was pacing and reciting, I was good, but as soon as I stopped it was all bad. I had to keep calm, because I wanted out of the there. I paced as long as I could before I got tired and lay down on the floor. I found peace in the smell of fresh air coming from under the door.

I don't know how long I was laid out in there asleep. I was awakened by the sound of an overnight staff's voice saying that I could come out and use the bathroom if I would do it quietly. I had been in that room all evening and most of the night, so I wasn't about to do anything to jeopardize me being out of there. After a long night of struggling to fall asleep on that hard floor, I was awakened again to the door opening. This time it was the morning staff letting me out.

I was so happy to be out of there! They felt as if it were safe to let me out since all of the kids were at school and I would be in the house alone. I can't tell you how happy I was right then...well, at least until I walked into my room. While I was in isolation, they took all of the stuff out of my room. They took the radio, the weights; they even took some of my notebook paper with my raps. I wondered why they would take my raps? I could understand taking the weights. They could justify that by saying I would hit somebody with them. I can even see taking the radio; it was kind of sturdy so I could have hit somebody with that, but my raps though?

I later learned that while they were cleaning out my room, they read some of my lyrics and got a little freaked out. "I don't care if I die, I'm going to live in the sky with Johnny." Even though that line connected my rhyme and had no hint of self-harm from me, to them it was suicidal.

Not only did they clear all the dangerous things out of my room, but they called my social worker, too! I was ticked off, but I couldn't do anything about it. The staff sat me down and had a long conversation with me. They wanted to make sure I wasn't going to start slamming people around again. I'd never had a real problem with Rob until that day, and I didn't have one after that day. After dinner, our normal routine would be to do chores and homework, and then TV if we had time, but that night I was pulled into another meeting with the staff. In most cases when a person starts off a sentence with the words, "We just want to say how much of a pleasure..." it's usually about to be all bad, and that's exactly how the sentence started. The conversation ended with the staff telling me that my caseworker had ordered me to be transferred somewhere else, and the people were already en route to pick me up. My plans to leave that place were for me to go home, not for me to go somewhere else. My life was again in someone else's hands and not my own.

I went to tell Ladonna what was happening, and to my surprise she really seemed to care. She didn't really care when her last boyfriend left, but there she was about in tears. We had spent so much time together, sharing our dreams and even making plans about what we would do when we got out of there at 18. A lot of those plans included us being together, so I could see why she was hurting. It was like something put us together for what seemed like forever, and then as soon as we got close, it tore us apart.

The time between us saying goodbye, me packing my clothes, and the staff from the other facility making it there was short. The funniest thing in the world, though, was that the staff from the other facility looked like the Lone Ranger and Tonto…no, for real. One was a Native American, and he had the whole long hair thing going on, and the other—well, you know how the Lone Ranger looked. The day staff did their best all evening not to discuss where I was going, so when I sat down with those guys I had no clue I was headed to a hospital. The staff shared the stuff I'd written in my notebook with my caseworker and the dudes who came to pick me up, mainly the part about me not caring if I die. When the two strangers sent to pick me up asked me what I meant, I told them, "I don't care if I live or die, where I'm from you're going to die or go to jail, and I don't care if I do either one of them."

Oddly enough, they completely understood what I meant, and I believed the Native American guy when he said he didn't think I wanted to kill myself. He then asked me a couple more questions about why I was acting out, and I told them what happened between Rob and me. He also asked me why I had an attitude with them right then, and with tears in my eyes I told him, "I just want to go home."

"I tell you what, Travis. If you come with us, do well in our program, and complete it without getting in trouble, we will talk to your caseworker about you going home." I didn't know anything about this dude, but I knew he was real about what he was saying. And let's be honest…I didn't have a choice anyway.

Once again, I was on my way to a foreign place, ripped from my home, my mother, and everything I knew. I just lay there, stretched out across the back seat of that van, headed to a place that I would be forced to call home for however long that they decided. That's when it happened—a part of me died. I decided right then, in what was probably one of my darkest hours, that I would be okay no matter where life landed me from then on. If this was my life, and I had more days of pain and hell ahead of me, I would never be out of control no matter where they sent me or how crazy life got. I would not be a slave to any situation.

The backdrop to my new situation was CPC Spirit of St. Louis Hospital in St. Charles, Missouri. The only excitement I had about being there was the possibility of going home. This was a straight up hospital! I knew they said I was coming to a hospital, but I didn't think it was going to be an actual one. While I was checking in, I got a chance to see one of the natives peeping out of the door to see who was in the hall. All I could see was his head sticking around the corner, but by the looks of it he was a young white kid about seven or eight years old. I wondered what in the heck a kid that young was doing there.

The room situation was different from Flat River. There, I slept in a room by myself, but here the rooms were four deep, and from the looks of it I had one roommate already waiting on me. I thought he was asleep when I got to the room, but found out fast he wasn't. "What's up bruh? My name is Roach, what's yours?"

"My name's Travis, at least that's what my momma told me all my life." The conversation started there and went late into the night. I found out that he was from St. Louis too, from Pine Lawn, and used to hang with my cousin from out there, Andrew. I could tell that Roach was one of those dudes who was cool to kick it with but could get you in all kinds of trouble, and if I planned on getting out of there on time, I needed to watch myself.

The daily routine there was a lot different. They woke us up around 8 o'clock; we got dressed, fixed our beds, and then went to breakfast. When we lined up for breakfast, I got to see every person in our area. Except for the small kid, we were all close to the same age. Just like Flat River, there was a boys' side of the dorm and a girls' side. The only difference here was that we had to cross the girls' side to get out of our area to go everywhere else. In Flat River we had to eat whatever the staff made for us, but here we had a buffet. No lie, we had a straight buffet! They had eggs, waffles, pancakes, ham, toast, and all kinds of stuff. They even had a juice machine with apple, orange and fruit punch, not to mention a soda machine with different flavors. I didn't know what the rest of my time here held, but this was a good start.

The kids in my group looked just like the kids from my old group, but the people in the cafeteria from the other groups looked like they were in a mental hospital. Some of them even had on hospital gowns and were walking slowly like they were doped up on medicine. After breakfast we went back to our section. We got to chill for a little bit, and then we went to this thing called "group therapy." I didn't know what was about to happen in there, but it was mandatory so I had to go or get written up. They had a level system there based on behavior, starting at Level 1 and ending at Level T. The amount of time it took you to complete the program was based off of behavior and rewards, so I needed to get my numbers up. My other motivation for not getting in trouble was their isolation room. It had a bed with straps on it and the staff had a dose of lithium waiting on you, and I was not trying to get doped up and tied down.

You know how those movie scenes are, with people sitting around in a circle in an AA group with someone saying, "Hey, my name is _____ and I'm an alcoholic"? That's what group therapy was like, minus the alcoholics. When the first person started talking, I wasn't even really paying attention to their words. All I could think about was how much it was like a movie and busted out laughing. Then I looked over at Roach, and he started laughing too. The counselor leading the group was ticked off! I could understand why, but I wasn't laughing at the kid talking, I was laughing at how the scene was set. She immediately put Roach out of the class and focused her attention on me. "So Travis, what part of this did you find funny?" I sat there with a smirk still on my face, trying not to laugh, and said, "I don't know."

"Well why don't you share with the group a little about yourself so we all can get to know you?"

"No, I don't want to share with the group, I'm cool!"

"Why don't you tell us how you felt about your friend Johnny getting killed?"

"Why don't you tell them since you know so much about it?"

The only thing they all heard from me after that was the door shutting behind me and my footsteps heading down the hall to my room. I couldn't believe that lady just tried to set me out in front of the group like that; what was she trying to do, make me wild out? I felt like it was the stupidest thing in the world, sitting in a room, in a circle, telling people your business like they were your family. The counselor gave me a couple minutes to cool down before she came to my room and asked me to come back. Even though I didn't want to be in there I went; but before I did, I made it clear I wasn't going to laugh but I wasn't going to talk either.

I walked back in with my mind made up that I would be involved in the group enough to get my levels up to get out of there, but I walked out with a totally different view. There is something about words that is so powerful and unstoppable. I may have been thinking too hard in there, but the thing about words is, once they go into your ears, you have no control over the effect they have on your heart. Sitting in that room, listening to those kids tell those stories about how crazy their lives were, made me realize something…my life wasn't as bad as I thought it was. This one girl was there because she tried to kill herself by crashing her truck into a gas station. She was so pretty, and she was only 18 years old, but when she talked she sounded so hurt. When she told us why she wanted to kill herself, I hurt too. Her father and her grandfather used to have sex with her, sometimes at the same time. After that class, I went back to my room and thought about my life in a totally different way. My momma had her issues, my daddy was gone, but there were people out there going through worse.

Life has a funny way of connecting dots. Back at Flat River, when the kids found out I was a Blood, they told me that I would have had some problems if this kid named Monty would have still been there. So guess who walks in my room to be my new roommate? That's right, Monty. He was nothing like they said. Dude was cool people. He said that after he left there, he had plenty of time to think about life and that gang stuff wasn't for him anymore.

Those daily group meetings got deeper and deeper by the day. I couldn't believe the stuff that those kids were talking about in those sessions. The stuff they were dealing with made my life seem like a Disney movie, and my life was quite the hell at times. Just when I thought I had heard all the crazy stories I could hear, we got another roommate who proved me wrong. When the light popped on in the middle of the night, we all knew that it was staff bringing in a new kid. He was a short, skinny kid with brownish red hair. He had a whole "elf" look, almost like one from a Santa Claus cartoon. It didn't take him any time to open up and start talking. The staff couldn't have been halfway down the hall when we knew plenty about him. The kid's name was Elton, and he was from the U.K. He was headed to his grandparents' home to live with them, because his mom was in jail for running a child pornography ring. The crazy thing was, he was one of the kids she used in her films. In the midst of all of this talk about child porn and things, Elton asked me where I got the troll from that was on my nightstand. The troll he was referring to was a stuffed animal that came from Ladonna. "He's not just any regular troll doll, he comes to life."

"Stop playing, what do you mean he comes to life?"

"He really comes to life, like me and you. When he does, he usually plays cards on my bed by himself." Anywhere else in the world, talking to a person old as Elton, I would have known there would be no way I could pull this off. But based on where we were, I knew there was a chance he would believe me. "Hey Monty, am I lying?"

"Nope, he comes to life."

"Kenny, am I lying?"

"He's not lying, bruh. You'll see; he's friendly though." It took everything in me to keep a straight face, but I had to because I wanted him to believe me. I knew this wasn't cool, but it was definitely funny and we were going to run this in the ground. Later that day, after dinner, we decided to take the joke even higher, and we did that with the help of the troll, some tape, and a deck of cards. I went down to the room, got the troll, sat him on my bed, taped a card to his hand, and set the rest in front of him like he was playing. While I was doing that, I sent Kenny and Monty to the sitting area to tell Elton that the troll was in the room playing cards. I hid in the bathroom so I could come out and fix him back fast to make it look like it never happened. When he walked in and saw that troll on my bed with those cards, he freaked out. He went running down the hall yelling for the staff at the top of his lungs, "It's alive, it's alive!" I came out of the bathroom, put the troll back in place, and got out of the room.

I walked down the hall holding my laughs in and went to the day room with everybody else. We all rushed to the hall when we heard Elton yelling in the hall, "I'm telling you, it was alive! It was playing cards!" Staff called me down to the door and asked me if the troll was mine, and of course I said, "yes" but when they asked me if it was playing cards, I looked at them like they were crazy. Elton wasn't going to let it die. I tried to give him a look like *chill out, man, it was a joke*, but he didn't get it. "I'm telling you, it was alive, it was alive!" The staff took him by the arms, and when they started walking him down the hall we all knew where he was headed…to the restraint room! He fussed and yelled all the way there until they hit him with that lithium, and then it was all silence and smiles. The other kids that had been in there said that lithium made you super high. There were even kids that got in trouble on purpose just so they could get high on it. They could have all the highs they wanted in that room, I was cool on that and the hospital. I did everything that they required me to do, and then some, climbing levels fast. Staff members told me it normally took students over ninety days to climb to Level T, which was the completion point, but I had made it there in a month and a half.

When those two guys picked me up the night I was transferred, they told me that if I made it through their program they would see about me going home, and they kept their word. After I completed Level T, I had an assessment. After the assessment and a call to my mother, I was able to go home the week of my fifteenth birthday.

CHAPTER 10
DWAYNE MINOR

I couldn't believe I was out of there and back in the hood.
It had been months since I'd seen my family or anybody in
the hood. A lot had changed in the months I was gone. I'd
gotten a little more size on me, had different life experiences,
and my little afro had even grown into some braids. Nobody
in the hood knew I was coming home, and I was anxious to
go surprise them all. After I had seen all of my family and
my homeboys, everybody knew where my next stop would
be…Monica's house. I crept up the steps and knocked on the
door. When Kandy opened the door she almost passed out,
she was so happy to see me. I had to stop her from yelling
before she ruined the surprise for Monica. Kandy let me in,
and I crept down the hall to Monica's room. When she saw
me, she dropped everything and ran to me.

The last time I'd been at Monica's house, my mom,
caseworker, and the police were pulling me out of there to
take me, as my mom said, "to get some help." Now, fast-
forward to me coming home months later. My mom was still
working, still in the new apartment, but I had a lot of the
"freedom" I used to have because she was back to some of
her old ways. For me, that meant I could get into just about

anything I wanted to. I was fresh home, so I played things a certain way because I knew the caseworker may be on me for a little bit. After a time, she was out of my life and I was right back at it.

Riding bikes and renting crack heads' cars was getting old fast. I decided it was time for me to hit the block, grind, and run my bands up (stack/save money) so I could buy me a car. It might sound crazy, but around here it was the norm. I'd watched all the big homies get dope rides at fifteen or sixteen years old, and if they could do it, I could, too. I didn't have a clue what kind of car I wanted to get. To be honest, I didn't even know how much cars cost; I just started hustling.

When it was time to buy, I didn't have to look far. It was like the car just popped up on me. One of my homie's mother had an old Ninety-Eight parked in her backyard. She'd stopped driving it when she got a new car, and there wasn't anything major wrong with it. We used to get dropped off at the skating rink in that car every week, so I knew how it rode already. I was joking when I approached Mrs. A and asked her if she wanted to sell it, but she wasn't joking when she told me "I sure do." When she told me that I could get the car for $300, I pulled the money out of my pocket right then and bought it from her. She went in the house, got the keys with the title, and I pulled it out of the backyard.

The downside to all the joy I had in owning a car was that I was only fifteen; I wasn't even old enough to get a driver's license. I didn't even have a state ID. I decided to worry about all that stuff when I had to, but right then I was going to show off my new ride. I stopped all over the hood, went and swooped Tank up, and we were rolling. Since I couldn't get a license plate, I came up with an idea—get some fake temp tags. I kept using the fake temps until my connect stopped selling them to me, and then I needed a new plan. I could have put it in my momma's name, but I knew that with all of the things I was doing, my momma could get locked up. I had one option left—throw a cardboard sign in the window that said "Stolen Plates." I had seen that on a car before, and based on the first couple times I got stopped, it worked.

My ride wasn't new, but the fact that I was fifteen with my own car made it seem like I was riding around in a Benz. I put some beats in it and had a good stash spot in it for the pistol. I would stash my ride in the cut all day, be out hustling by bike or on foot, then I would jump in the car at night, usually on a mission messing with some girl. Girls loved to come in the hood; no matter how dangerous it was, they loved being out there. We would have straight-A school girls coming down there all the way from the county in their momma's cars, because they loved the trap boys.

Having a car had its benefits. I didn't have to wait for anybody to take me anywhere; I could dip when I wanted. But, it also had its downside; my enemies had something to identify me by. Once we started banging, it didn't stop. By this time, The Martanna was one step away from being the baby Carter. We had started doing so much crazy stuff over there that my Uncle James decided to sell the building before somebody got killed. Before they shut The Martanna down, we set it off. The last months there, we basically ran the building on our own. All of the adults had left, and it was just teenagers there. Every day was a party. Our front porch was set up like it was made for the type of missions we would be on. There were five feet concrete posts on each side of the porch that looked like they were made to duck behind for protection and to take shots at people.

Letting your guard down in the midst of a war zone is something that can cost you your life, and that's something that I almost learned the hard way. Tank and I were sitting on the porch talking when I decided I was going across the street to shoot dice. I knew he had a clear view of everything coming either way, so I was good. This night my luck was on; I was hitting everything I was throwing! I was hitting tens, nines, eights… everything I threw I was hitting! My cousin Ortez was over there too, and we were both hitting. I shook the dice getting ready to roll when I saw a group of dudes out of the corner of my eye. The direction they were coming from, I figured they had to be cool because Tank would have seen them first and stopped them, so I didn't even trip off them. I stayed focused on the game.

Something in me said to turn around and look, and when I did, I saw four dudes lined up on the sidewalk with pistols aimed right at us. Instantly, I saw sparks. "Bow, Bow, Bow, Bow, Bow!" There was nothing for us to hide behind, so instinct had to kick in quick! It was happening so fast but at the same time it seemed like slow motion. The dudes who lived in the house ran in and slammed the door—suckers! I was looking around, getting a full view, and then I saw a way out—jump the porch rail, hit the gangway, and run through the backyard. When I jumped the rail, my plan didn't play out the way I saw it in my head, because my cousin jumped the rail in front of me and I landed on top of him in the gangway. As I hit the ground, it became obvious real fast that the only thing between them and us were the two trash cans sitting there. I had to grab Ortez and calm him down. "Be still, Cuzz! Stop moving; if you don't want to die, stop moving now!" We lay still, and after the shots stopped it was just as quiet as it was before. The silence was broken when people started coming to their doors, calling out names to make sure their people were okay.

The whole time I was lying in the cut I was thinking two things: One, don't let these dudes figure out we were right there, and two, where was Tank? I knew he didn't freeze up, that's not in his DNA. I also know they shouldn't have made it that close to us at all. We got up out of the gangway and ran across the street. As we were hitting the porch, Tank was running down the steps with no shirt on, no shoes, holding his pants up. "Cuzz, what happened?" we both asked each other. While they were out there trying to kill me, he was upstairs with his girl! That night, Tank gave a new meaning to the phrase "getting caught with your pants down."

It's crazy how you can get used to just about anything. As humans, we have something in us that helps us adapt; well, some of us, at least. It's a proven fact that when some people endure trauma, they black out in a sense, or go to a place mentally that helps them survive what they're going through. By nature, we have something in us that clicks on and helps us survive by any means necessary. The first time you get shot at, your brain says, "If I get hit, I could die." After surviving the first time, your brain says, "If I don't get hit, I'm going to live." I decided I wouldn't go anywhere without a gun again. I was in a war zone. The downside, you can't have a war without casualties, and it hurts when you take a loss. We'd lost Leo, Gus, Johnny, and even a homie named Chris. He was murdered in the project's hallway, trying to go see some female.

Up until this point, we had taken losses, but it was older homies. One summer day, my life would change forever. I was standing on the corner, using my people's phone, when I saw a car coming down the street toward me. It drove up, slowed down a little, and then the driver smiled at me and kept rolling. I couldn't make out the driver, but I could tell he knew who I was by the way he paused. I kept talking, and not even two minutes later I heard, "POW, POW, POW!" Looking down the street, I saw the same car that had pulled up in front of me sitting in the middle of the street and there was someone on the ground. I hopped in my car and pulled down the street so I could see who had been shot. I pulled up and saw Dudda looking shook, with his hands on his head. Then I saw Gee and that's when it hit me …Wayne! Where was Wayne? Wayne was laid out in the street, shot. He was still breathing, but gasping, in short breaths.

Time froze and everything went slow. I felt like I could hear my heart beating. I don't even remember who it was, but all I remember is somebody talking to him, saying, "Breathe, man, hold on. The ambulance is on the way." You could hear the ambulance in the distance, but Wayne didn't look like he would make it until they arrived. His breath starting getting shorter and shorter like it was getting harder for him to breathe. He had been shot, but there wasn't any blood coming out; you could see the hole in his stomach but no blood. His stomach started to swell up and his breath got even shorter; he was bleeding internally. I stood there over my little homie and watched helplessly as he gasped, gasped, gasped, then breathed his last. The look in his eyes…he didn't look scared, he didn't look sad. He wasn't saying words with his mouth but his eyes said a lot to me. When the ambulance pulled up, they tried to revive him, but it was too late. They put him on the stretcher and his arm fell off to the side. He was gone! My little homie was only thirteen years old, and I just stood there and watched him die in the street like a dog. How do you go tell a mother that her only son just got murdered? That's some news I'm glad I didn't have to deliver. I wasn't even a drinker, but that night I got wasted. I couldn't believe that the homie was gone like that.

I woke up the next day wishing that what had happened the day before was a dream, but it wasn't. It was real. The pain I felt was real. The anger I felt was real. When it rains, it pours! The added salt to the wound already open from Wayne was that Dudda got locked up and couldn't even go to Wayne's funeral…his best friend and he had to miss it. He'd gotten locked up because he was driving some of us around in my car, and we'd gotten pulled over. Besides the fact that I had a cardboard sign in the window that said "Stolen Plates," I don't think the police were happy to find a fifteen-year-old owning a car. Couple that with a thirteen-year-old, Dudda, driving and you had one ticked-off policeman. The police cuffed Dudda up and told the rest of us not to leave there driving or I would go to jail too. He gave me a break, because he could have towed my ride. My little cousin, Worm, and I sat there so long waiting on the officer to get out of the area that I dozed off. By that point, I didn't care if they caught me or not; I jumped in that driver's seat and dipped.

Looking down on your homie in a casket is not easy to do. It hurts! It hurts badly! Wayne's death was the kickoff to a crazy summer. Bodies started dropping all around the city, and I wasn't trying to be another number in the murder rate.

CHAPTER 11
ONE LIFE,
ONE DEATH

It's crazy how time can fly by when you're out in the streets. I guess that's why they call it living fast. It seemed like yesterday I was sitting in the fifth grade, anxious to get outside and play. The days just fly by, then the weeks, and then the months. One second it was March and the next it was October. Before I knew it, I'd be somewhere, sixty years old, talking about "remember when we used to do this." That is, if I made it out of the jungle alive. As long as you're alive, you will have hard times at some point—it's almost certain. You can't escape it. At sixteen, I had a whip, was grinding and trying to stack my paper, then there I was, a few days from my eighteenth birthday, broke, with no ride.

My little cousin Worm had a way of getting under people's skin like no one I have ever met in my life. We were sitting in the hood on the trap front, and I was almost flat broke. So, what did he do? He pulled his little money out and flashed it on me, even flashed his little work. He knew no matter what he did, I wouldn't do anything to him because he was my little cousin, but he also knew how far to take it to before I got to the point of wanting to do something to him. "Peeps, what's wrong with you? You're out here straight broke! How are you broke and I got money? You're the one who showed me how to hustle!" As much as I didn't want to hear it from him, he was right. It was time for me to get back on my feet. I had $50 to my name, and I wasn't going to move from that spot until I came up, and that's just what I did. Fifty turned to eighty, eighty to this, this to a quarter, quarter turned to a half. Three days and very little sleep later, I had turned that $50 into $3,000. I was back on my feet, and I wasn't trying to be broke again anytime soon.

In every hood around the world, you have the same types of dudes, just different names. You have the hustlers, the dudes that are about getting money. You have the players; the players are usually weed heads, too, because they smoke with seven or eight different girls, a few times a day. The players usually aren't good hustlers, because they spend all their time with females so they have no time to get money. The players usually aren't gangsters either, but some of them can fight, because they're always into it over some other dude's girl. The gangsters don't need a breakdown; they are the muscle…the hitters, the dudes that hold hood order, inside and out. Then you have the bottom of the barrel. The sneaky, scandalous, do anything, nobody trusts them, "homeboys." They're one notch over the crack heads; all they do is stir up drama, steal, lie, etc. It's smart to keep them far away as possible.

One of my favorite people to hang around with at that point, besides Tank, was my homie Famar, a.k.a. Dirty Red. Famar was a straight ladies man. The homie was a heavyset, light-skinned, ole Heavy D-looking boy, and the girls loved him too. The funny thing was, he loved big girls and nothing but big girls. One day I asked the homie what was it about big girls that he liked, and he said, "I don't know, man, I just love them. There's just something about them that I love. I can't explain it." I really didn't care because that was my family and he could like whatever kind of girl he wanted, as long as she was ride or die.

On my eighteenth birthday I planned on kicking it hard! We all knew the rules: no matter how many girls were around, on the birthday, holidays, or any other important days you had to kick it with the main, and my main at this point in life was Rachel. We'd been messing around for years, and I was the only dude that she had ever been with. Everything in me wanted to do right by her, but everything in me also wanted to do what I wanted to do. I tried my best to keep my mess away from her, but sometimes I was messy and it made it to her door. When I first met Rachel she was a virgin, so I never pressured her about sex because I knew she hadn't ever been with a dude before. Most cases when I chilled with her at her house, we hung out and watched TV. If she came to see me, she'd hang out, then I would take her back home. The girls I messed with in the streets were already out there like me. They were hood. They'd be in the club like me and some of them even hustled like me. Rachel was different from us, and I didn't want to mess her up.

I woke up the day of my birthday, not feeling eighteen at all. I knew another thing that I wasn't feeling anymore—walking. It was time to get a whip again. I grabbed some cash and had a crack head take me around to some car lots, looking to see if I could find something nice. After riding around all day, I found it, a burgundy four-door Cutlass. I had to have it. It didn't take a lot of negotiation to get the keys for a sweet price. I drove to the hood, parked the car in front of our hood house (place where we hung out), and walked to the park where my cousins were. We walked back from the park, and I couldn't wait until we got within viewing-distance of my new baby. As soon as we could see it, somebody asked, "Whose car is that in front of the house?" and I proudly said, "Mine, birthday present to myself."

When I first started hustling, I didn't get high, but then I messed with it a little bit here and there. When I did, I had one rule: I wouldn't get high until I was in the house for the night, because I couldn't afford to be outside high and get caught tripping. That rule lasted for a while, but it wasn't long before that was out the window. All it took was one time for me to hit a blunt while I was out in the daytime and it was over. There were always people around me getting high way before I ever started, and they were smoking more than weed. Many of them were still making money while they were high, so I figured if they could do it, so could I. Between trying to get to the money and all the crazy beef I had going on, I didn't have time to be pausing and getting high anyway, so most times I didn't. I stayed posted on the block, day in and day out, no matter what day of the week it was. As long as money was coming, I was there.

Life was going a certain way, and I was happy with that way. But, life will throw you a curveball when you're not expecting one. Rachel had always been a person of few words until she was mad or something, so when I got a call from her saying that she needed to talk to me face-to-face, a part of me knew something was up. She swooped down on me, I hopped in the car with her, and we rode to her house. I could tell something was wrong, and when she started talking, her words quickly confirmed my assumptions. "Travis, I'm just going to spit it out. I'm pregnant."

All I could think was, *I just messed up this girl's life. She doesn't need to be pregnant by me.* My next thought after that was, *Her momma is going to kill me!* As much as I wanted to give her what she wanted from me—faithfulness—I never could give it to her. But, because she was standing there, pregnant with my baby, I would try.

My family loved Rachel, especially my girl cousins, Felecia and Thunder. I was always around them both; Fee and me would be together so much, people who didn't know us thought she was my girl. They both tried to help keep me in line, and I was trying, but for the new girl, Tameka, that had just moved to my block, I was willing to make an exception to that rule. The first day I saw her walking down the street, I watched her all the way to the mailbox and back. The next time I saw her out, I tried to talk to her, and she didn't give me the time of day. It was cool, though. I'd be patient and wait until the opportunity presented itself.

There was one girl in my life that I could not seem to get away from, KeKe. No matter how far apart we would end up, something always brought us back around each other. I hadn't seen her in months and had no idea where she was. That was her specialty. She knew how to disappear when she wanted to. I was on the north side, hollering at some of my people, when I ran into KeKe's sister, Sherry. She was always super cool, even when her sister and I would be at each other's necks. She told me KeKe had moved and that she was about to have another baby. I thought nothing of it and kept it moving, because I had to meet somebody else back in the hood. As I was getting in my car she said, "You know who she's pregnant by, don't you?" "No, I don't know who she's pregnant by, who is it?" She said, "By you."

"MAN, HERE WE GO AGAIN!" I couldn't believe it… here I was, just finding out about Rachel being pregnant, and now I hear this. Talk about timing. It was eight months since

I'd seen this girl, and that whole time she was pregnant and didn't even tell me? Her sister wouldn't tell me where she was, because she knew KeKe would get mad. Let me make it plain how crazy this was. I had just been told that I had a girl pregnant that I hadn't seen in 8 months. I had to go and tell my main, who was 6-months pregnant, that I'd gotten someone else pregnant, too.

That conversation was one of the hardest ones I've ever had. She came to the door and stepped outside to talk to me, belly so round all I could think was, *My baby's in there.* I didn't want to hurt her, especially while she was pregnant, but I had to tell her. "Look, I'm just going to blab it out. I just found out that I got another girl pregnant, like eight months ago."

"What do you mean, like eight months ago? As in, she is eight-months pregnant?"

"Yeah, she's eight-months pregnant, but I swear to you I didn't know."

"Wow, so she's going to have your baby before me? What's she having?"

"I don't know. The only reason I know she's pregnant is because her sister told me. I haven't even seen her in like eight months, I'm not lying to you." She was hurt. I was hurt too, because I knew she was hurt, and as much as I did my thing, I didn't want her to leave me. She shocked me with her response and how she handled it. She looked at me and said, "I forgive you. Don't let it happen again." My mouth said it wouldn't, but my mind, body, and actions knew it would!

It was Christmas Eve; I was fully dressed and ready to hit the club, when I got the call that Rachel was in labor, about to give birth to my son. This little dude picked a perfect time to come to this messed-up world. My biggest fear in having kids was that they would grow up to be like me—or they would be in this world on their own because I'd be in jail or dead.

Too late for all of that now, here we were. "Push, breathe, push, and breathe." My son wasn't out the womb before he started having trouble. The doctor told us that the umbilical cord was wrapped around his neck and was messing with his breathing, so they had to get him out right then. I had never held him before or even seen his face, but I was so scared that he was about to die. I didn't want anything to happen to my son. He was all I had right then that gave me hope of some good in the world. We pushed, and we pushed until he was out!

They took him over to the table and started to work on him, where we couldn't see. He was out for a few minutes, and I was nervous because he hadn't made a sound. Then, the fearful silence was broken with the crackle of his little voice crying out, "freedom!" That little voice gave me a reason to live. It was like he was saying, "Daddy, I need you." When I held him for the first time, I studied him. He was skinny and long, colorless, like most babies, but the backs of his ears were black. I said to myself, *Dang this boy's going to be dark!* I had never seen a woman have a baby before. Women are some tough people! I could not believe that she had just gone through all of that and was still alive; I would have died right then, first push.

It wasn't long before Rachel was out, as she should have been, and I did the same. Except I wasn't out asleep, I was out the door and headed to the club. I went back to the hood, swooped up Tank and Lo, and we hit the east side and kicked it hard. We stayed in the club so long that the sun was coming up when we left. Merry Christmas! The next day, my joy was still on high at the birth of my new son, but it also gave me something else to think about; I may have another son that I have never seen. I didn't even know where he was. I couldn't believe this girl would go so hard at hiding from me while she was pregnant. I had to find out where she was.

By the time my son was born, I was into so much crazy stuff that I wouldn't even let him or Rachel ride in my car. I couldn't even drive my son to the doctor, because I refused to get into some pistol play with my son in the car. It was a necessary precaution, because if something happened to my baby, I would've tried to murder the whole city. The streets will pull you into situations that make you do things totally against your heart. The people that you loved, that you thought you were out there to help, you were really hurting. I swore by it daily, that I was out there getting money to take care of my son, but because I was out there all the time, I barely saw him. His momma swore I was out there spending all my time with other girls, and that was partially true, but she didn't get it; she wasn't out there. It wasn't always a party, sometimes, most times; it was hell out there. I was in a situation at least once a day that could've cost me my life. I sat in my car for hours one night, thinking about that kind of stuff, and at the end I decided to do right. I wanted to be there for my son and my girl.

I drove over to her house and sat out front, thinking even more. I was about to go in and tell her I was sorry for all the dumb stuff that I had put her through, and that I was ready to try to change, for real. I had this whole idea in my mind how this was going to play out. I walked to the door, euphoric in a sense. I knocked on the door and walked in. The room was full of some of her family members as usual—momma, sister, aunt, cousins—but there was some dude sitting there that I'd never seen. I had been around her forever and seen all of her cousins, so I knew this wasn't her people. I walked over to my son's car seat and picked him up to hold him.

This part of the picture was playing out like it did in my head: I was holding my son; he was looking was up at me and I could feel his love… but the thing that happened next hadn't been in my plans. Rachel's cousin looked at her and said, "Dang Rachel, I didn't know you were a player like that, got two men over here at one time." I turned around and looked at little buddy, like *oh yeah?* and then I looked at Rachel. She didn't have anything to say, no words, so her mom did the talking. "She doesn't have two boyfriends; one is her baby daddy and one is her boyfriend."

I was heated!!! Good thing I left the pistol in the car! Rachel sat there and didn't say a word. I don't know if it was because that's her normal, if she was scared, or if she didn't care. What I did know was that if I stood there any longer, I could do something I may regret. I put my son back in his seat and walked out of the door. I didn't say a word to anybody because I knew if I did, I would end up saying something crazy. I went back to my car almost in shock. I couldn't believe my little quiet girlfriend that I'd always thought was so innocent ended up playing me. I went back to my car and had some crazy thoughts: A) kill him; B) kill him, or C) the same as A and B. Truth told, he had nothing to do with the situation; it was between her and me. On my way there I had wanted to settle down and all of that fairy tale stuff you see in the books, but that just proved to me that it was not how my life would be. Back to the regularly-scheduled program.

By now my weed smoking was way past just at night. I was into so much beef that my enemies hated me and the police were itching to catch me doing something. No matter who I didn't want to ride in my car, I couldn't keep Felecia from riding or driving. The police would pull her over and try to get her to tell something on me, but it did no good, my cousin was ride or die. I guess luck was just on my side, because no matter how hard they sweated me, they never found anything, even though I kept a gun on me. In St. Louis, bodies were dropping like flies and I was not trying to be another number in the year's murder rate. I would rather get caught with it and sit in front of a judge and jury, than be carried out of a church by six of my people.

My luck with the police and my enemies was put to the test more than once. I was in so much crazy stuff at one point, that every night I slept in the living room with the chair pushed against the wall by the front door. I wasn't just sleeping there to welcome everybody that came in. I slept there every night with a 45 automatic. If somebody kicked in there looking for me, I would be the first person they'd see and my family wouldn't get harmed. I slept with that pistol, I ate with that pistol, and everywhere I went I had that pistol on me.

There was a police officer in the hood we called "Batman." We called him Batman because this guy thought he was a superhero. He was always rolling up on you, trying to talk like he was your friend, but in the life we lived there were few friends, especially the police. I walked out of the house one day, hopped in my car, and while the car was warming up, I sat there with the pistol on my lap. Out of the corner of my eye I saw a police car pull up beside me, and guess who it was...Batman. He and his partner were so close that our doors were almost touching; I was boxed in. There was no way for me to get out of that car. "Travis, what's up man? You shot any Crips lately?"

"I don't know what you're talking about Batman, you know I don't do stuff like that." Now picture this scene: two policemen in a car, with me blocked in. The policeman on the driver's side could just jump out and run around the car, but I would have to climb over my seat. By then he'd be waiting on me, most likely with his pistol in hand. In my head I had two options in this scenario: 1) if Batman got out of his car I could sit there, wait for him to come around and look in the car, see the pistol, and I'd be off to jail; or 2) I could take my chances shooting it out with them, hoping to get away. As much as my mind was racing and thinking about what I should do, my body language was composed as if nothing was going on at all. We sat there and talked for at least ten minutes, the whole time me with a pistol on my lap. When they pulled off, I couldn't believe what had just happened. I laughed so hard; if they only knew.

Gunplay and street life go hand in hand, so if you're out there and active, there's usually a pistol close. There are some people who are just as dangerous to themselves with a gun as they are to someone else. Famar was one of those people. He was always messing around with a gun, especially if he was high. Guns don't discriminate on who they shoot, bullets don't have GPS, and if one hits you in the right place, then it's lights out forever. We knew that firsthand all too well. It had been three years to the day since Wayne was killed.

Every year since then, on that day a group of us would always go to his grave spot together. We'd just sit around and talk, chilling like we were on the block. In the midst of all our stories that day, Famar came out and said, "The next time we come back up here, one of us won't be here."

I was like, "What do you mean?"

"The next time we come up here, one of us will not be here. I just have that feeling, one of us will be gone." Everybody was like, "Man, you tripping, stop blowing highs," and we went back to what we were doing.

Every hood has those crack heads who used to be a goon before they started smoking, but still think they're hard. We had one of those named Reggie. That fool Reggie used to do karate or something before he was a smoker, and he still thought he had Bruce Lee skills, but that dope took the power out of those kicks a long time ago. He had his days where he would buck all the way against authority. He wouldn't get too wild, but he would make his, "I'm not these other crack heads" statements, like we wouldn't do anything to him. He was so far from wrong. The only reason Reggie got as many passes as he did was because his people were from the hood. A part of me was waiting for him to get out of line.

Famar would always be in some feud with those crack heads, so it was only a matter of time before he and Reggie clashed. Everybody knew that Reggie thought he was the last dragon, and this day he was really talking crazy to Famar. I'm not going to lie; I was egging it on a little. "Famar, are you going to let this guy talk to you like this? You need to put hands on this guy." I was waiting on him to go ahead and swing on Reggie so he could get the beat down that he'd been asking for. Right when I thought it was about to go down, Famar—in classic Famar fashion—pulled out his pistol and pointed it at Reggie. "Man, what you are doing? You're going to shoot this crack head out here in front of all these people and go to jail, over a crack head? You tripping!" When Famar turned to respond to me, Reggie saw his window and took off running like Usain Bolt. When he took off running,

Famar took a couple shots at him but he missed. I told Famar, "Man, you're soft for shooting at that crack head, you should have whooped him."

Famar looked at me and said, "If you're my boy, you should have my back regardless of what I chose to do!"

"I did, that's why I wanted you to whoop him!" Having disputes with my homeboys wasn't anything new, but this was the first time we had ever argued to the point that we wanted to throw blows. Famar and I didn't talk for days, and I was feeling some type of way. I was riding back to the hood on a late night mission and saw Famar on his porch. He was knocking on the door, leaning, barely able to stand up; he had to be blowed. I needed to talk to my dawg and apologize, tell him I was wrong, I should have been with him no matter what, and if I wasn't, it shouldn't have come out that way in front of all those people. I paused, hit my brakes, started to back up, then thought, *I'll holler at him tomorrow.* At the corner, I felt the need to go back, so I turned around. I needed to go connect with my brother and get things smoothed out, but by the time I made it back by his house, he'd gone in.

I woke up the next day feeling good! I went to the store, bought a cooler, got some ice, and filled it with drinks. I didn't even drink beer, but I knew the homies did, so I copped it for them. I got to the hood, found some good shade under a tree, and posted up. The way the day started, it felt like it would be one of the best days in history, but the look on Gary's face when he was running up to me let me know it was about to be crazy. He was running for his life, and the words that echoed from his mouth made my heart drop. "Famar just got shot in the head!"

Time froze! *God, I can't lose my dawg, not right now, we have too much to do. We didn't even finish our rides*

145

yet. Whoever did this is going to pay! When I made it to the hospital, I found out that the shooter and the person I was worrying about were the same person. Famar had accidentally shot himself in the head. We had told this dude over and over about playing around with them guns. We told him that he would learn the hard way...but I didn't want my dawg to learn like this.

It's crazy how a single bullet can snatch the life out of a person, and here my dawg was laid lifeless. Just the week before we had been racing in our cars through the hood. It was just the night before that I saw him knocking on his door. MAN, I should have stopped the first time I drove by. They had the homie hooked up on a breathing machine, wires and tubes going everywhere. I couldn't stand to see my brother like that. When a person is on life support, no matter how much hope you have, you also know there's a chance they will never wake up. By the end of that week the homie had swollen up and everybody in the room thought it was over. Sitting there looking at him, all I could think about was when we were at Wayne's grave and he'd said, "One of us won't be here next time." This couldn't be the end; I needed the homie to wake up. I needed to apologize for the stuff I had said that day. One of his family members decided that we should pray, so we all gathered around his bed, held hands, and somebody prayed. As we've all heard before, "when it's your time to go, you go," and nothing can change that. I guess it was his time to go. When they unplugged him, his girlfriend said, "Look, he has a tear coming from his eye." But, the doctors said it was fluid from all of the treatment, that he couldn't be crying because his body wasn't functioning on its own.

That was it; the homie was really gone, and the last time we'd said anything to each other, we were arguing over something petty. I was already wilding before Famar died, but after he died I turned all the way up. Even though he had shot himself, I wanted everybody to feel the pain I felt about his death.

The world has a way of throwing you some hope in the midst of crazy situations. The last I had heard of KeKe being pregnant or anything had been months before all of this. I didn't know what had happened, but I knew somewhere I had a son I wanted to see…two for that matter. Since I had gone to Rachel's house and had seen her there with her new boyfriend, she had been on a straight mission with my son and would not let me see him at all. I guess she thought him being there would make me come begging that she take me back or something, and when I didn't respond the way she wanted, she did the only thing that she knew would hurt me—keep me away from my son.

As I said, the world has a way of throwing you a bone, and this bone came in the form of a phone call from KeKe's sister. Needless to say, I wasn't expecting a call from KeKe's sister and definitely wasn't expecting her to say that I could see my son. I don't know what her logic was for running off, but at that point I didn't even care. I had missed his birth, and he was now seven months old, so no telling how much more I had missed. *Is he going to look like me? Is he healthy? Does he cry a lot?* I had 100 questions going through my head. All I wanted to do was hold him, and when I walked into her sister's house, that's exactly what I did. I picked my little man up and it was crazy…it was like staring at my own face but on someone else's body. As ticked as I was that she had kept him away from me for all those months, I didn't want to say anything that would make her run off again and keep my son from me. I had lost enough. Growing up around there, we learned fast not to hold on to anything too tight, even life, because you could be dead any minute. But sitting there holding my son made me want to live. It made me want to live for my kids.

CHAPTER 12
ART IMITATING
LIFE

Whenever we sat around getting high, nine times out of ten it would lead to my cousins and me free styling, especially when my cousin Drew came through. It would be us versus his squad. My cousin Drew was a straight hustler. Drew had been in the streets so long...he was put on house arrest when we were in the sixth grade. Not only was Gutta a hustler, he would get high as a kite; he smoked that juice or, as most called it, water (PCP). Every now and then he would try to get us to smoke with him, but I wasn't messing with that juice. I smoked a dip one time and was not a fan of how it made me feel, so I wasn't in line to get on it again.

When I was fourteen years old, I started growing my hair and got it braided. I hadn't had a haircut since, so my braids were long. When I found out that Tameka, the girl I had noticed when she moved on the block, knew how to braid, I decided that was a way to get close to her, at least for the time she was braiding my hair. She wasn't dumb though, she knew what I was up to, but she still did it. She already had a boyfriend, and from the outside looking in, you would think he was a cool dude. But, the more I talked to her, I found out he wasn't. Somewhere after our first conversation,

I went from wanting to try to get in her pants to wanting to protect her from this guy, but I knew it really wasn't my business. I learned early growing up that you stayed out of relationship beefs. You'd jump in the middle of them, trying to help somebody, and they'd both end up jumping on you. My auntie had it bad. Her boyfriend would put his hands on her, I'd come beat him up, and she would be right back with him the same night.

This dude had Tameka on a mission. She was sneaking out of the house, staying gone for days, and getting into big trouble with her momma. Her momma would let her know about it, too, right on the front porch when she got back, in front of everybody. He would do what dudes like him do— drop her off and pull off before she made it to the porch. I knew her momma hated this dude. Her momma loved me though, just like all the other people in my neighborhood. The only people who saw my bad side were my enemies. To my foes I was a nightmare, but to my family and friends I was an angel, no matter how many stories they heard.

The more Tameka and I talked, I found out most of the trouble she was getting into wasn't by choice. That dude was taking her hostage. When she would be gone overnight, it was because he wouldn't let her go home. He popped up a couple of times while she was braiding my hair, but he didn't have anything to worry about, because she wasn't messing with me. As messed up as that clown was, she was still faithful to him, and I did not understand that. There is only so much that the most faithful person can put up with before they make an exit, though, and Tameka finally reached her limit with that guy. He was gone.

When Tameka and her family moved in, we just knew that there could be all kinds of crazy problems with her people. The last thing we expected was a Hood vs. Hood football game, that had our park looking like the Cardinals playing the Rams. Honestly, I didn't understand it at all. Any other time we would have been this close to each other, we'd have been trying to kill each other on sight, but there we were playing football. It was only right that we won the game because it was in our hood. After the game was over, we all ended up on the block in Tameka's backyard, drinking, eating, and getting high. Again I couldn't explain it at all, but it was happening.

I don't remember exactly how it came up, but somebody in the crowd asked, "Do y'all got somebody from your hood that rap?" and of course all the homies said me. They were convinced that, unlike the football game, they would walk away with a "W." I didn't know what or who they had up their sleeve, but I was up for the challenge. The homie Feez pulled his car in the alley, popped the trunk and cut on beats, and we went at it. Their homeboy was dope, but you could tell he was spitting already-written rhymes and I was going off the top of the head. I was used to spitting rhymes for hours with my cousins, but this was different. I was being judged on all angles. After going back and forth four or five times, he spit a rhyme that was so dope, then just walked off like, "Yeah, I won." I don't know if he really thought he won, though, because the look on his face said, "I'm running out of verses," but either way no matter what he thought, I felt like I had lost.

As soon as we finished, an OG from their hood named Ray Ray walked up to me and said, "You didn't lose, he just had songs. If you would have had songs it would have been different, but you still didn't lose. You killed it." Right after that, Tank walked up to me and said, "You have to start writing songs. I've heard you write verses with all bars and no hook, but the hooks, that's what does it. I need to hear you write some songs with hooks, you need hooks." I felt both of them. Before either of them said it, I felt it. I knew the only thing he had on me was hooks and songs.

That battle woke me up. Before then, I was just free-styling and not really tripping off writing, but I went back to writing whenever I could. Even when I would freestyle after that, I pulled a dope part from the bars I was coming up with and made it into a hook. It made it seem like a song; even when I was free-styling, I seemed prepared. I went on a championship run after that, taking on all challengers. I even hit the studio and recorded a couple of songs, some solo and some with my cousins. I had the hood going crazy; everybody was listening to my songs.

Music wasn't the only thing I was taking a little more seriously. Tameka wasn't just braiding my hair now, she had been my girl for some time, and we'd just had a beautiful daughter named Treneece. She was the most beautiful person I had ever seen. I couldn't believe that I had something to do with making a person so beautiful. Her little curly hair, her chocolate skin…I knew that if I could, I would give her the world. Some days I hated to even look in the mirror because I didn't like the monster that I saw looking back at me. But when I looked at my baby girl, I saw a part of me that was worth loving.

I had a big homie named Jerome who was from across Martin Luther King, from the same hood as the biggest local artist in St. Louis at the time named Los. I can't front, I was a fan of Los and his label Bullet Proof Records. When I bought my first car, it was the first album I bought to play in the car. Their music was hard. When I first heard them, I couldn't believe that they were from St. Louis, because they didn't sound "local." Jerome would come to me, popping off about how dope Los was and how he would go get Los to shut me down. One night I was on the block talking about music with Jerome and Feez, and of course Jerome started going in. "I'll go on Arlington right now and get Los. He will smash you."

My answer was the same then as it always was, "You can go get whoever you want." Jerome pulled off and went to Arlington to get Los, but couldn't find him, so he came back with nothing but the same threats. The next day Jerome swooped up on me on the block. "I was making sure you were out here. I just saw Los, you still want to battle?"

I answered back, "Yeah, go get him!" Honestly, I didn't think J would come back with Los, but to my surprise, he pulled back up not only with Los, but with half of the Bullet Proof artists—even the producer D-Red. When I first saw Los, I was in that *dang I can't believe this is Los, I bump his music in my car* zone. I was walking over to him to show respect, say, "what's up," you know, keep it 100. That's when he opened his mouth, and fan-mode was gone. He said, "Is this the dude right here? Come on, man, so I can get this over with." I looked Los straight in the eye and said, "Before you said that, I may have gone easy because I'm a fan of your music, but now, that's out of the picture!"

Here I was again, on my block battling another rapper, and the whole hood was out. When I say the whole hood, I mean the whole hood, everybody from old ladies to little kids; people were walking over from the next block. He came at me the same way ole boy did in the backyard, with songs he had written, but this time I was ready for that. I had songs too, but what he wasn't ready for was, I could freestyle and it sounded like songs, but people knew it wasn't because I was talking in real time. I would spit my bars and everybody would go crazy! It got to the point that all of the rappers with them jumped in. I was battling the whole label, and then Dudda slid in out of nowhere and we shut it down. Everybody out there was turned all the way up. It was like I didn't just win for me, I won for them. I won for the whole hood. We shook it up when it was over, and I gained Los' respect. D-Red even gave me his number and told me to come through their studio to check out some beats.

Los had the reputation of beating everybody, so when the dudes that ran Bullet Proof heard about our battle, they could not believe it and had to meet me. The first time I went to D-Red's studio I thought I was just going to listen to beats, but it quickly turned into something else. Every beat he threw on, I spit bars to it, and killed it. His big brother BJ couldn't believe it. He kept trying to get D-Red to throw me curve balls, but it didn't work. I rocked them all, all the way down to a reggae beat. They couldn't believe what I had just done, but for me it was normal. I was used to sitting around, free-styling for hours at a time. It was like a fish in water, my natural space. That night, in that basement, not only did I spit over twenty-plus D-Red beats; something between us clicked, and we started putting in work on the music.

As much as I loved music, two things kept me from doing it. First, trapping, because no matter how good of a rapper I was, I had mouths to feed. My babies couldn't eat mix tapes. Second, if I couldn't do music with my cousins, I didn't want to do it at all. It was either take them with me, or no me; that was the deal. When I told D-Red that, it didn't stop him from wanting to work with me, and whenever he could get me in the studio, we made magic.

Tameka told me that when her momma moved to a new apartment, it was going to be a one-bedroom with partial disability living, so Tameka and my baby couldn't move with her. Her mom had already worked it out with the landlord so that we could stay there and pick up the rent, all we had to do was say, "Yes." As much as I hated the idea, I knew my baby needed a place to live, but I did not want her having to live with me in the very place I did my dirt. At first, I stayed away from my front porch when doing business, but once people figured out where I lived, especially the smokers, they were at my door all times of the night.

Between trapping, getting in the studio with D-Red, and all the beef I was in, my summer was crazy. Music was always secondary, because the streets put up situations that demanded immediate attention, but with Los in jail and Bullet Proof killing the streets that summer, I was working both ends of the candle. Life was moving super fast. One minute I'd be in my hood on some full-blown trap stuff, and the next minute I'd be on a stage in front of a couple thousand people. The grind was serious; because I was in the street so much, in most cases I would write and record my verses the night before the show.

I worked as hard in the studio as I did on the block, and I learned how to work fast. When I got in the studio, I could write a song in an hour or less and have it memorized by the time I was done. D-Red and I were literally up all night recording verses, rough mixing, and ready to ride the next day. My first time up rocking a big crowd, the whole city seemed to be there. I wasn't even on Bullet Proof's label, but they showed me all love. I appreciated the love and opportunities, but it wasn't complete for me because my cousins weren't on stage with me. The train was rolling, but instead of embracing it, I tried to jump off several times.

When females see guys that they respect, they want to be a part of that. No matter what made me mess with different girls in the street, none of them could make me leave my girl and my daughter. I lived to come in that house every night to wake my baby up and play with her. I would sit and talk to her like she was old enough to understand, and she would sit there and look at me like she knew what I was talking about. I would often be in awe that I'd had anything to do with making something so beautiful. She was the prettiest thing, especially when she started talking. She might as well have been speaking Chinese, because I couldn't understand a word she was saying, but it didn't matter.

At one point I became like this "rap" hit man for everybody around me. Drew rapped himself, but even he would come get me on some "Unk, I need you to kill somebody for me; he thinks he can spit." One night we ended up on the north side, at a spot where a bunch of dudes from his hood hung out. I'd been over there a couple of times and had met most of the dudes there. Midway into me spitting one of my verses, in walks Shaun Holmes, a guy Drew knew, that I hadn't seen since we were little kids. Even though I hadn't seen Shaun, I had heard about him. Anybody in the streets with two ears had heard about him.

When I finished my bars, he was super-hyped. I gave respect, said, "thanks" and "what's up," but I wasn't a male groupie. Money didn't move me, because I could get my own bread. What I didn't expect for him to do was spit a verse, and I definitely didn't think it was going to be dope. But it was; he actually had bars. "That was dope, Homie, you can spit." The way Shaun responded and Drew looked at me when I said it, let me know Shaun had rapped a hundred times and had heard a hundred times that it wasn't cool. The fact that I liked his flow gave me an instant place with dude. Me and Drew rode with Shaun on what ended up being an all-night mission.

Shaun and Drew grew up together. At one point Shaun had stayed in Drew's mom's basement, but I didn't really know him. Dude was super cool, and you could tell he was just happy to be around some real dudes that he could be himself with. I could only imagine being around all the different people he dealt with who'd be trying to get close to his money; always having to watch out for the feds or the jack boys trying to put a bullet in his head for some petty money. I didn't have those issues. I got money in my hood with my family, and I knew any one of them would take or give a bullet for me without even thinking about it. I could let my guard down around my family and know that I wouldn't end up tied up in some empty building, getting beat until I told where my stash was. Shaun couldn't, not until then.

The next day when he showed up on the block, I knew he was just happy to be around some real guys. Money can buy a lot of things in this world—cars, women, houses, clothes, jewelry—but no amount of money in the world can buy you loyalty and respect. That's what Shaun came to the hood for; he knew I was loyal and he respected me, as I did him. When Shaun came around, he'd throw parties any day of the week. We would hook up—Shaun, Thunder, Dudda, Drew, Tank, and I would get together and kick it hard. Of course, when you put so many people in the same room together that rap, it would eventually turn into a rap session.

From this, we became Fambino. One of the most notorious mob families in New York history was the Gambino Family, named after mob boss Carlos Gambino and later made famous by John Gotti. We wanted a name that said two things: One, we were family, because we were; all of us were blood family except Shaun, and by that time he was like blood. Two, we wanted a name that said that we weren't playing, this wasn't a rap group, we were a gang. Fambino fit perfectly—equals who would lay it down for each other.

The problem with Fambino was that the realness that we all rapped about kept us from doing music. Shaun was all over the city, Drew was in his hood, and the rest of us were on the west side. Over the course of time, some of the big homies from our block were killed and some went to jail. Those events left the block in the hands of our squad, with Tank and I at the head. Things were different around the hood; the whole hood was still our block, but each section had different squads on different parts. You had the homies on P & H, you had the old heads that hung in the park, you had Primo with his squad in the Gardens, and our squad on Bartmer.

We went anywhere around there we wanted and posted up anywhere around there we wanted, but from the way it looked, the homie Primo didn't understand Family. The Family was the original name of the hood before Bloods, because that's what we were, family. The fact that he was from the hood made me hope that the stuff we started hearing, and the way I was feeling about him weren't true. This guy wasn't one of my enemies on the outside of my circle, trying to catch one of us tripping out in traffic; this was someone that, by hood rules, was my brother. We had smoked together, fought together, rode for the same block for years, and even buried the same homies. He was supposed to be family. Anybody else, there would be no question about the consequences for being a threat to the family, but I didn't want to believe that about my Primo, and neither did Tank.

As much as I didn't want my house to be a trap spot, that's exactly what it had become, and the traffic was getting way out of hand. It wasn't a problem for me while I was there, because I could handle it, but the thought of somebody running up in there on my girl and my baby was something I didn't even want to think about, much less see happen. To add to the situation, Tameka was pregnant again, and the last thing I wanted was to bring another baby home to live in a trap house. I couldn't let this go on any longer, so I got them out of there and into a new place where nobody would know how to get to them.

Once they were out of the hood, it was on. Things were going good so fast, but one day I had a persistent thought when I woke up. I remember telling Tank, "It's crazy, I woke up today, and I had this strong feeling that I need to get my hair cut. I have a feeling it's going to get me in a lot of trouble." I could not shake that feeling. It was heavy! My hair hadn't been cut in over five years, so I had long braids past my shoulder. Tank and I talked it out and then went on about the day. That night was just another night in the jungle, but I did keep my word—I went and got my hair cut off.

Tank had this saying—"We got the respect, we got the power, now all we need is the money," and everything was rolling that direction. In the hood, we celebrated as hard as we mourned. When our brothers and sisters fell, we mourned them hard, but we also celebrated their life, no matter how short-lived. On our birthdays and for the births of our children, we celebrated even harder. On August 31st that year, we had twice the reason to celebrate. My second baby girl was born. We named her Tamia Latonya Tyler. She was just as beautiful as her mother and sister. She also shared the same birthday as one of my other favorite girls, Thunder, and now they even shared a name, Latonya. That night we kicked it hard!

On the ride home, dropping Tank off that night, we had one of the deepest talks we've ever had. One of the things I told him was, "Sometimes I can't see past today. I can't see myself living to be old. I think about my daughter and I can't even see her face, I can't see my daughter getting older. It just looks black to me. Cuzz, I think I'm going to die or something."

That conversation stuck with me all night. I didn't get any sleep. It was like the whole vibe had changed. The next day, that thing was still riding me. I needed to talk about that junk again, so I couldn't wait to get to the hood to see Tank. When I made it to the hood, he was the first person I saw. He came walking from behind my old house, and headed straight to me.

Tank walked up, grabbed my shirt, looked me straight in my eye, and said, "Cuzz, it's not you, it's me. You're not going to die; I'm going to die. But you, you're going to help change the world! Whatever happens to me, don't you stop rapping! People are going to listen to you: Asian people, African people, Mexican people...you're going to help change the world." After he finished naming all of those people groups from all around the world, he started rapping a verse to me that I had done with D-Red:

Come to my world and see if you can find a solution/
On how to end guns, crack, bombs, and pollution/
Aids, cancer, deforms, poverty, prostitution/
Tell me what to say to make my people start to regrouping/

Tell us why the police kill us now-a-days when they swooping/
And everything that's going on falls back on the youth and/
The whole world thinks we're wrong 'cause we're living illegal/
They act like we hear no evil everything we see is evil/
Turn on the news you'll see the president shooting bombs/
Wounded kids, crying tears, bodies lying, bloody arms/
Foreign languages translated my whole family is gone/
Then we turn the other way like we don't see what's going on/
We're doing the same thing y'all doing, just in a smaller space/
The only difference is we're killing off our own race/
All the things that we've been through, physically and mentally/
For the past 400 years you'd think we'd stand together for one century/
Form gangs in the penitentiary, form gangs on the street/
For us all to form a gang takes one of our people to be beat/
We turn our women into freaks don't care if our own kind don't eat/
As long as our pockets stay fat and our clothes stay neat/
I think deeper than the average but I can't seem to figure out/
I know I'm tired of stressing on it I'm just gone go and live it out/
Feels like I'm fighting a title bout and I'm twelve rounds down/
But I'm trying to catch my breath to go twelve mo' rounds/

I've been up, I've been down, I've been happy, I've been sad/
Had a few good days but hard 22 years bad/
After all of this I found that I could just be me/
And try to learn something off of everything that I see.

I remembered back to when I wrote that verse in the studio. I said to everyone in there, "I didn't write this."

Even though I had lived most of my entire life in a four-block radius, I believed Tank when he said that I would help change the world. Something inside of me believed him, I didn't know why but I did. He had a look in his eyes that I had never seen before, like he had seen something...something I hadn't ever seen, something that had convinced him.

Over the next week, every night I dropped Tank off, we would have talks similar to that one. He told me that I was too smart to be out in the streets, that I had a brain and could go anywhere or be anything. He also told me that I needed to stop waiting on my cousins and go pursue music on my own. Out of everything that we had talked about or I had heard him say that week, that was by far the strangest thing, because we were family or nothing. He knew of all the things and opportunities I had turned down over the years with different people because I couldn't do it with family. He also knew that they didn't want it like me and that it would only hold me back, that I needed to go get it for myself. I never thought I would hear Tank say, "You're going to have to leave them," but then again I was talking to the realist dude I've ever met in my life and he was going to keep it 100 regardless.

No matter how hard we tried to ignore the issue with Primo and hoped for the best, it kept coming back up. I didn't want to keep assuming or going off of hearsay, because there were several people in the middle and I knew how that could go. So, I went to talk to the homie. Sadly, after talking to him, I had reason to believe what we were hearing about him. He didn't say too much at all, I did most of the talking. He just drove and listened, but the vibe he gave me said it all. A few days later, he and Tank had a conversation about it too, but their conversation didn't go anywhere nearly as peaceful as ours had.

I couldn't figure Primo out. What was it that he wanted? We had basically taken him in like family, and we had love for this dude like a brother, but that wasn't enough. Where was it coming from? I guess he wanted to be the king! I didn't know what was happening to homie, but whatever the issue was, at that point I didn't have time to figure it out. My job was to keep my blood safe.

I went to talk to Tank so I could get the firsthand info from him about what happened between him and Primo. After what I heard and the way we live, there was only one thing left to ask. "So what are you going to do?" Tank answered, "Nothing."

"Nothing?" I didn't understand, because at that point it was obvious that the situation was past the point of reconciliation on Primo's part. "Tank, for whatever reason in this dude's head, he feels like he wants you dead."

"I'm not doing a thing to him. Before I have the whole hood hating me for killing my own brother, I'll let him kill me first." As much as I didn't agree with his answer, I understood it. We were cut from a different cloth than Primo. In our minds, we were still The Family, and the people who loved us, loved him. We loved his sister and brother like family, our friends were his friends, and vice versa. All of the people who had sat in front of their houses and watched us grow up had watched him grow up. I hated Tank's answer, but I understood it. You don't kill your family; you don't kill your brother.

It was always funny to me that even though I wasn't pursuing music, I was often presented with opportunities to do big shows and open for national artists. I remember my first big show…it was a dope memory. I was nervous, excited, a mix of all kinds of thoughts and feelings, and this show felt special. I was on stage, rocking the crowd, opening up for one of the biggest artists out, and up front I saw Tank. I could hear him over all the noise of this two thousand-plus crowd, cheering me on. It was like his yells were translating to me, saying something totally different. It was simple yelling, but not to me. To me, he was saying, "Cuzz, go and get it. I'm proud of you, I see you. I'm here." We kicked it so hard that night. It was a perfect celebration, all the way up until we were walking out of the venue. To funnel a couple-thousand people out of a single opening at one time was hard enough, then add to that a large percentage of them being drunk, and you have an entirely different problem.

As we were finally walking out, a dude decided to sneak and grab my home girl's booty. The dude directly beside her may not have been the person to do it, but because it was so packed he was the closest person to her, so that's who she turned around talking to. When she yelled at him, he said something back, she busted a beer bottle over his head, and we all started brawling. We managed to make our way to the car without getting caught up by the laws. Tank was already at the car when we got there; he didn't even know we had been fighting. When he found out that we had been fighting, he was ticked. He was so heated, he just started trying to pick random fights with everybody walking past.

We were all still so hyped, we didn't want the night to end, so we hit the bridge and went to the east side to go to a club. By the time we got there, the energy of the car had changed. Tank's liquor had worn off and everybody else's had kicked in. As we got out of the car, people were saying the same thing, "I don't know if I want to go in now, I'm faded." Tank looked at me and said, "I just want to kick it. I just feel like kicking it," and again the look he gave me said that this dude knew something I didn't. I wanted to kick it with him, everything in me knew I needed to kick it with him, but we were out-numbered on the vote to leave.

September 16, 1999. I had no way of knowing, when I woke up that day that I would never forget it for the rest of my life. We'd been going so hard over the past months... heck, for the past year, that the night before caught up with me. I was home early and out like a light. When I woke up, the word was shot to me that during the night, Tank was with Shaun, and some dudes that Shaun had an issue with had shot at his whip. No one was hurt, so that was good, but that still didn't mean it was cool to be shooting at The Family. We needed to meet up and pow-wow. I called Thunder's spot so I could get the word on what really happened, and she filled me in on the details. Before I hung up with her I asked where was Tank, and she said, "He's right here headed out the door. Do you want me to stop him, you want to holler at him?"

"Naw, I'm good. I'll holler at him when I come out." I was still so tired. I had been asleep all night, most of the morning, and I was still dog-tired, so I went back to sleep. I don't know how long I was out, but I slept good. I woke up to Tameka standing over me, handing me the phone. "Here, it's Dirty."

"Dirty, what's good peeps?"

"I'm outside with Feez; we came to pick you up. Something happened, but I'm going to let your people tell you."

When he said that I knew. "It's Tank, right? Is he dead?" And Dirty said the words that I didn't want to hear but I knew were coming...

"Yeah, peeps he's gone." It was unreal. Even with the entire dialog we'd had over the past few weeks, I was not ready for this to happen. This was my dawg. I couldn't imagine life without this dude. I had to pull it together for my family, my hood; they were going to need me to be strong. I had to get out there to see what was going on. When I got to the car and found out that Primo had done it, I did not want to believe that. The whole time I was upstairs getting dressed to head out, I just knew that it was somebody who we were beefing with, somebody who had valid reason, somebody that we had done something to, not this guy; not our own family.

The way the story was told, one of the little homies was in The Gardens talking crazy to Primo, talking about we were going to come down there and shoot up The Gardens. They got into a tussle, and the little homie ran down the block to the corner store. Primo went in his house, got a chopper (AK-47), jumped in a car, and went looking for him. When Primo saw him in front of the store, he jumped out on little homie and for whatever reason didn't shoot, but tried to hit him with it. They tussled again, the little homie got loose to run around to where we posted. When Primo pulled up on the block, he jumped out of the car, talking out loud but at no one in particular. When he pulled up, Tank got up and started walking off, not even responding to what he was saying. Until this point, even though no guns had been pulled, no physical threats had been made, I can only imagine Primo thought it would still get ugly. So he turned to the only person out there that he feared could end his life, Tank. He turned to Tank and said, "What's this I hear about you saying you're coming down to shoot up The Gardens?" Tank stopped walking and looked back at him and said, "If I was going to do anything to you, you know it would have already happened." At that moment, something clicked in Primo's brain, and he started shooting.

My phone was ringing like crazy. Everybody in my family was calling me because they knew how close we were, and they knew what type of mission I was about to be on. When I made it to the hospital, so many of my family members were in that waiting room. I walked to the back room, the small one where they allow immediate family to view the body, and Tank's daddy, Fred, opened the door for me, weeping hard. "He's gone, Travis. He's gone. Our boy's gone; they took my boy from us, our boy, he's gone." Seeing Uncle Fred so broken up killed me. I looked around the room and everybody in there was just as broken up as Uncle Fred was…Maudie B his momma, his sisters, his kids' mother, everybody. I walked over to the table they had him lying on. There he was, stretched out on the table, white sheet covering his lower body. He laid there lifeless. The most painful cries that I had personally heard in my life echoed off of the walls of that room. I stood over my cousin, my friend, my brother, knowing that nothing I could do would get him up off of that table. My legs gave out and I lost all power. I hit my knees, my mouth opened and from deep inside of me I yelled, "God, why, why did you let this happen, WHY?"

I'd always heard people say don't question God. I didn't know why they said it, or if it was in the Bible, because I didn't read the Bible. But, I think when I asked God those questions in that room, He was listening.

I sat on the window's edge in Maudie B's living room the following day after Tank's murder, looking around at my family, their hearts full of pain and their faces soaked from tears. As I sat there I felt something, almost like I heard it whispered to me, "This is what you have been doing to people for years." At that moment, I looked around the room and saw it in an entirely different way. If this was how we were doing people, I never wanted to see anybody hurt again.

I don't even remember certain parts of Tank's funeral. I don't remember who preached or what the preacher talked about. I don't remember what anyone talked about, not even me. I was out of it. All I remember is when they lowered his casket in the ground, it felt like they lowered me in there, too. The days were short, the nights were long, and I had a front row seat watching the whole hood stumble over the rubble that was left from the bomb that had rocked us all on September 16, 1999.

CHAPTER 13
GUILTY UNTIL PROVEN INNOCENT

I had always believed God was real, but had never prayed as much as I did during that week. There was nobody around me that I could turn to for answers about what had just happened. The only place or should I say person I could turn to was God. Everything in me was hoping that God was listening and that He would answer me. I was headed to the hood on a Friday night; I still hadn't gotten my swing back. I was still hurt, still angry, and still looking for Primo with no luck.

When I turned the corner to our block, I saw people everywhere. People in groups, people on porches talking, people in the street, on the sidewalk, people everywhere. I rode down the street, parked in front of Feez's house, and hopped out to see what was going on. I wasn't out the car two minutes before one of them came over and talked to Feez and I, but you could tell he was super nervous, which he had the right to be. Talking to him, we found out that all of the people out there were from the church up the street. They came out there that night to pray and talk to people after Tank's murder. I walked up the block and posted up in front of my old house.

This old head walked up to me and asked how I was doing. I knew he was trying to make small talk to pull me into some kind of conversation, but I entertained it anyway. He asked me my name, I told him. Then I asked him his, and he said, "Pastor George White, Jr." Pastor? I couldn't believe this dude was a pastor. I'd never seen a pastor outside of a church before. Add that to the fact that this dude was wearing jeans, a name brand jacket, and tennis shoes. He asked me, "What do you do besides be out here?" I had been out there all of my life, it shouldn't have been such a complex question, but it seriously made me think. After a few seconds of thinking, I said "I rap," and then he asked me to rap for him. This pastor did not want to hear me rap, I was more than sure of that; he was going to have to get baptized again after hearing my bars. Then it hit me. I said the rhyme for him that Tank quoted to me the day we had that talk. Not only was it the only song of mine that I could think of, it was the only song I had that was preacher-friendly. When I finished rapping, he complimented my flow and asked me if he could introduce me to some rappers from his church.

Church rappers? That's what I was saying in my head. What in the world could some dudes rap about from a church? I had no idea what to expect, but I walked with him anyway. The only reference I had in my head was Kirk Franklin's "Stomp," and I hoped they were not about to break it down on the block like that. Pastor White introduced me to a group of three dudes called "Due Season," and I can't front, it was way better than I thought it would be. When they finished their song, one of the dudes in the group said, "You should introduce him to Flame."

They took me over to the dude named Flame, and I remember thinking to myself, *This dude looks just like us.*

If I saw him on the street, I would never have thought that this dude was a "Christian." After we were introduced and we shook it up, dude spit some bars for us. I had never heard anybody rap about God, or even talk about God in a way that I understood so well. He rapped about God with the same passion that we rapped about the trap. I leaned over and told Dudda, "This dude raps just like us, except he's not cursing." What I meant by "he rapped just like us" was that it was real; you could feel it. This dude was so convinced that God was real; it made me question how real God was for me.

The church invited everybody that hung around to hear them that night to come back to the church for refreshments. There were a few hundred people from the church, walking, clapping, and singing the same song. I felt like I was in a movie, on one of those freedom walks or something. Pastor White invited me out to church the next Friday, too. They were having a service just to invite us back.

When that next Friday came, I mobbed up to the church with some of the little homies and sat in on the service. I met the dude Flame again and got a chance to rap with him a little bit. It felt good to go to church. A part of me didn't want the service to end, because I knew how crazy it was outside, and in there it was so peaceful. I wished that peace would have followed me back outside to the trap, but it didn't.

A few days after I went to church, the police were all over the city looking for me. Their reason—I was the number one suspect in a murder. As soon as I walked out of the house and got in my car, I wasn't in the hood long before my granny called me, fussing in my ear. "Travis, baby, what have you done?"

"Nothing, Granny. What are you talking about?"

"The police just left my house looking for you. They said you've killed somebody!"

"What? Granny, I haven't killed anybody! The police are looking for the wrong person. I promise, Granny, I didn't." I wasn't off the phone a minute before my granddaddy called; they had been to his house too. Then I received a call from my momma, saying people saw me on the news. This was crazy! I got out of the hood and went back to our apartment so I could tell Tameka what was going on. When I walked into the building, the dude who lived across from me met me in the hall. "Man, you better get out of here. The police just left, looking for you about a murder. They just walked out. I'm surprised you didn't run into them. They had a picture and all, but it didn't look like you now. In the picture you had braids." Whoever told the police where I lived didn't really know, because the police didn't go to my door. I went in the house quickly to talk to Tameka. I got her and the girls some clothes packed and took them to my momma's house until I got things figured out. I had no idea what was going on, but one thing I knew for sure, they were looking for me everywhere.

I didn't know who they thought I had killed until I got back to the hood, and when I found out who they thought I killed, I was crushed! The police thought I had killed my own boy, Marcus. When the situation happened with Primo and Tank, it put a wedge between some of the homies, so it was easy to understand why they thought it, but I would have never done anything to hurt Marcus. I loved him, I loved his momma; we were like family. The homie had nothing to do with all the crazy stuff we did in the hood. He drank his beer and talked his talk, but big bro wasn't a street dude. I was hurt for cuzz, but right then my life was on the line. If it were something I had done, I would have been a step ahead of this, but this caught me so off guard. So, I did the only thing I could think of at that moment—I called Pastor White.

I went to the church to meet up with him, told him what was going on, and he told me he would make some calls to try to find out what was happening. After about an hour or so, he hit my line and told me that the police were looking for me, which I already knew. But the crazy thing was, the homicide detective who was looking for me used to be Pastor White's partner. Pastor White used to be a policeman. He told me that he talked to his former partner and also told him that he believed that I didn't do it, and that he would bring me to turn myself in. I told Pastor White I was cool with that, I just needed one day to get some stuff situated.

CHAPTER 14
FREEDOM

I knew how murder cases went…innocent or not, it could take me up to a year or two before I'd get a trial. Even then, with a criminal record like mine, piled onto the fact I was black and a known gang member, the court would take a free throw if it meant getting me off the street. With all that in mind and then some, I wanted to make sure some things were straight before I turned myself in. When I left after talking to Pastor White, the first thing I did was go to hire a lawyer. Even though I was innocent, I knew the system wasn't going to believe me, so I was making sure I was straight.

My big homie, Paul, and I rode out to Clayton to a law office, looking for this certain lawyer everybody used for serious criminal cases. If he could get dudes off the hook that had committed crimes, I knew he could get me off since I didn't do it. Once at the building, we found out that the lawyer we were looking for had moved offices. All we were left with was the list of lawyers on the wall directory. I looked over the list and said to Paul, "I'm going to go to him, Travis Ryan, he has the same first name as I do." Paul and I went up to Travis' office and asked his secretary if we could see him. I found it strange that she just sent us back to his office without thinking twice, but what happened next blew my mind. We walked into his office, and before I could even get a word out, he looked up at me and said, "I don't know what your case is, I don't even know if you have any money, and I don't care. Whatever your case is, I'm going to take it for free. When you walked in here, something just told me not to let you leave here without helping you."

I was blown away! I hadn't ever seen this man a day before in my life, and here he was making a commitment to me that most people wouldn't even make for their family. I sat down at the desk to talk to him, and as promised, he agreed to take my case for free, even once he found out what my case was. I gave him all of the info I had, which wasn't much, because I still didn't really know in full what had happened. Travis wanted me to wait two days until he had finished some prior court commitments. At that time, we would meet and he would take me to turn myself in. But I wasn't having that. "I'm innocent. I'm going to turn myself in tomorrow. These folks have been to my granny's house, I'm not going to have them going back to my granny's house, and I didn't do anything." Travis is a lawyer, so of course he understood the law a lot better than I did. He told me that if I turned myself in, they would lock me up for that murder, innocent or not. Even though I knew what he was saying was true, I wasn't about to run from something I didn't do. The following day, I would go with Pastor White to turn myself in, and Travis told me when I did to call him, because I'd be locked up.

The next day I went to the church, parked my car in the church parking lot, and went with Pastor White to turn myself in. I knew I was innocent, so I hoped to go in there, say what I had to say, and walk back out. But they did exactly what Travis Ryan said they would…read me my rights and locked me up. Once the interrogation started, I found out all of the details, and of course it made me feel even more that I would be going home. But they were convinced I was guilty, no matter how honest I was being.

Every night over the weeks since Tank's death, I would be out all night, go home, then pass out, unaware of anything at all; but, the night of the murder they were accusing me of, that wasn't the case. Usually when I got home, either Tameka would be asleep or she just would not say anything, but on the night in question, as soon as I walked in she said, "Hey… what time is it?" That made me look at the clock and tell her what time it was. All the nights before that, I'd stay in the living room by myself, but that night she came in there with me and lay down with me. When I told the detectives that I was home way before the time they said the shooting happened that night, and that Tameka was there with me, they brought her in and questioned her too.

By the time she got there, I had already been there for hours in the same room, and they were still asking questions. Once they questioned Tameka and let her go, they came back in, questioning me some more. At one point, the detective asked me how long it would take for me to get my hair braided and I told him I wouldn't be able to get my hair braided, because my hair was too short. I told him I had it cut off over a month before and it would be awhile before it grew long enough again. In my head, I was tripping out, because the main thing running through my head was when I told Tank, "I am going to get my hair cut. I have a crazy feeling it's going to get me in a lot of trouble," and here I was now, being questioned about a murder by a detective who was obliviously looking for a suspect with braids.

They asked me every question they could, then even hooked me up to a lie detector machine and asked them again. After the second lie detector test, I was super frustrated. I had been asked questions for hours by then, and no one believed me. The dude giving me the test said I failed the first two, but he was giving me another one, like I was stupid... if I had failed, why were we taking another one? He had the nerve to ask me, "Why are you getting mad, is it because you're guilty?" I told him, "No, I'm mad because I've been in here for over twelve hours, answering the same questions over and over again; I'm tired physically and tired of being accused of something I didn't do." After the last lie detector test, that I also passed, another detective came in to talk to me. He said the longest they could hold me without issuing a warrant was 24 hours. They had already held me 21 hours; if they didn't issue one in three hours, they had to let me go.

It didn't take another three hours for them to get that warrant. It seemed like he walked out and came right back in with a warrant and read me my rights. Once in the cell, I sat there in disbelief. I spent the whole night thinking that out of all the things I had done in my life, I was now in a cell facing the possibility of life in jail for a crime I didn't commit. It was hard to believe that there was a chance I would watch my kids grow up through monthly visits and pictures. I had taken lie detector tests and even had an alibi, neither one mattered to them; they just wanted me off the streets. With my criminal record, going in front of a jury was a scary thought, innocent or not.

I didn't tell anyone what I was there for. I didn't have time for one of those guys to try and cop a plea, making up lies about me, so I spent my time there by myself, waiting on court. I hoped that I would be going home after appearing in court, but I also knew that the reality of that happening was slim. I had a little more hope of going home once I saw how the judge was handling everybody else that came to court from my dorm. The court clerk would call them to the front, read off their charges, the judge would ask them if they were guilty or innocent, and then would either say 'time served' or offer a bond. Now granted, I wasn't stupid; I knew my case was serious and no one else had stepped up there with a murder charge, but I was still optimistic.

When the court clerk called my name, I stepped up to the judge's desk. With everybody else before me, the judge had asked them, "How do you want to plead, innocent or guilty?" But when I walked up, she said, "Travis Tyler, you are being charged with first degree murder, first degree armed criminal action, unlawful use of a weapon, and first degree breaking and entering." I thought she'd never stop reading charges. When she stopped reading charges, she didn't ask me a thing. She looked up at me and said, "You have no bond, talk to the clerk about your next court date, and I'd advise you to get a lawyer," and then banged her gavel.

I yelled and asked her, "Your honor, don't you want to know if I'm innocent or guilty?"

She said, "Get a lawyer. It will be determined during a trial if you are guilty or innocent." So there it was. Travis Ryan was absolutely right, those folks didn't care if I was guilty or innocent, and they were going to lock me up regardless. It made sense for the system—they had gotten one of their "problems" off of the street. I couldn't believe that they had me hemmed up in there for something that I didn't do, and that it could take me as long as two years to prove I didn't do it. I called my momma when I got back to the dorm so I could tell her what happened, and so she could call my lawyer. Now that I knew I'd be there for a while, or forever, I needed my momma to come get my property and put some money on my books. As soon as Travis got word from my mom, he sent the senior partner from their firm, John Sandals, to come and talk about my case.

John told me, "Travis couldn't make it because he's in court." He also knew that Travis had agreed to take my case for free and was on board with that decision. John asked me the same question that the detectives asked me about my braids. I told him the same thing, that I had them cut a month or so before, and he asked me for the number of the person who had cut my hair. We talked about my bond; I didn't have one, so they were going to try to get me one. Mr. Sandals had even talked to my grandfather, and Granddaddy said if he needed to, he would put his house up for my bond. I couldn't believe that. Granddaddy was always super tight about that bread, and there he was, willing to put his house up for collateral. He definitely believed I was innocent.

When Mr. Sandals and I finished talking, they took me back to my room. The first thing that came out my mouth was, "God you got me for something I didn't do, but you got me. Guess I'll be preaching in jail." I thought to myself, *What is going on, why am I thinking like this?* Me, preaching...I had only been to church once, that was crazy! I immediately started pacing. I had a lot on my mind. Maybe this was, as people would say, "me reaping what I'd sown." I'd done a lot of wrong stuff in this world, and maybe it was all catching up to me.

But, before I could get too far into my reflection, that's when it happened: God spoke to me. It wasn't verbal, out loud, audible speech; but I could hear it clear as day. "Pray, and I'm going to get you out!" What I heard wasn't spoken with words, but it was so real that I spoke back verbally. For years I had believed God was real, and even though I knew this was real, I didn't want to hear it and my words confirmed that as they echoed off of the 8 x 10 cell walls. "God, I've been praying all my life and I am still here right now. This is where praying has landed me. I'm cool on praying for right now."

Again, I heard, "PRAY, AND I'M GOING TO GET YOU OUT!" The second time was just as clear as the first time and even more real, but I still didn't want to pray.

"God, praying is not going to change anything. I don't have time to pray right now."

Yet again I heard clear as day, as if God was in that cell with me, "Pray, and I'm going to get you out, right now." With nowhere else to turn and a presence around me that I couldn't ever remember feeling before, my resistance broke and I hit my knees.

"God, you know I didn't do this. You know I have done enough stuff to be in here the rest of my life, but I didn't do this. God, I'm not going to say what I will or won't do when I get out of here, but I will say this: from now on, when I know You're speaking to me, I will listen, and I will go wherever you send me. Amen." I rose up from my knees and felt like a weight had been lifted from me. I lay down on my bunk and went to sleep. I hadn't really slept since I'd been there, and after the prayer I slept peacefully.

The sound of the CO (corrections officer) tapping on my window and calling my name through the door's intercom broke my sleep. I hopped up, expecting to be moved to a long-term housing dorm since court was over. I grabbed my bucket (item you're given to hold your possessions like toothpaste, socks, etc.), walked to the door, wondering where I would be placed. "CO, what dorm am I going to?"

"Dorm? You're not going to a dorm, you're going home."

I just knew this dude had made a mistake, or he was playing the worst joke in the world on me, and I didn't think it was funny.

"Come on CO, you know what I'm in here for. Why are you going to do me like that?"

"I'm not playing, with you Tyler, you're going home. You've been released." He extended his arm out and showed the slip he was holding that said I was free to go. I COULD NOT BELIEVE IT! My emotions were a wreck. I wanted to cry, I wanted to yell. Thankful doesn't even begin to explain how I felt.

I walked out of that cell and asked every CO on the unit "Is this for real, are they letting me out?" I rode the elevator to get my property, I even asked the COs down there. I couldn't believe it! When my momma made it to the jail to get my property, they told her to wait because I was on my way down. She didn't know how I was getting out, so she called Travis Ryan, and he came around to see what had happened. I had never been so happy to hear a door close behind me or to see my momma before in my life. She was equally as happy to see me, but she could not believe that I was out. When she called Travis, she thought that he'd gotten me out, but he was just as shocked as she was. When I walked out, the first thing I saw was Travis hopping out of his little sports car and running over towards me with the biggest question mark written all over his face. "What happened? How did you get out of there?"

Even if I wanted to tell him something different, I only had one truth to tell him. "I prayed, and God got me out!"

CHAPTER 15
WHY AM I HERE?

There is a scripture in the Bible, Proverbs 21:1, that says, "The king's heart is a stream of water in the hand of the Lord; He turns it wherever He will." I don't know how the story played out behind the scenes, but this scripture makes it plain that God can pull the strings of man's heart to complete His will. I had just walked out of a courtroom, after standing in front of a judge, with felony charges, no bond, and a court date.

I told Travis again, "God got me out," and I would tell anyone who asked me the same thing, because that's the only truth I had. "God got me out."

When I saw Tank lying on that table in the hospital with his head laid back and mouth open, blood on his grill, no life left in his body, I thought to myself for the first time, *One day I'm going to die and when I do, if God is who He says He is, I'm going to see God face to face. If God is who He says He is, He gave me this life.* And for the first time I thought, *What is God going to think about the way that I have lived my life?* It became obvious to me, looking down on Tank's lifeless body, that he wasn't really a "Tank," he wasn't invincible, and neither was I.

I had always believed God was real, but I also had a twisted idea of who God was. My granny used to tell me, "God knows everything." So, I believed that if God knows everything, then He knew that I was going to live in that crazy neighborhood. He knew my daddy would be gone and that my mom would be fighting a drug addiction. So, if God knew all of that and God was in control of everything, then He knew I would have to trap (sell drugs) so I wouldn't starve, right? If all of that were true, He also knew that I would have enemies who would try to kill me and that I would have to protect myself, right? All of my life growing up, I really did believe God was real, but because of the way I believed, I also believed God was cool with everything I did. Way before being in that cell, when I found myself in some of the worst situations and miraculously escaped them, I knew it was God or a thing I know now as God's common grace.

What about the time I was driving to my cousin's house, higher than a Russian Space Station? I was so high that I couldn't fix my rearview mirror. I was missing exits, swerving, and I had no idea how I was going to make it to where I was going. I was gripping that steering wheel so hard that it should've snapped in two. The entire time I was praying, "God get me there safe, I will never do this again." Guess what? I made it there in one piece, GRACE!

What about the time some of my enemies waited for me all night to come out of my house and when I pulled down the street, they shot my car up? In the mist of it, I heard that voice. It was as clear as day and because it was, I listened. It said, "DUCK!" As soon as I ducked down, a bullet busted my back window. I made it to the hood, looked at my car, and whoa! The bullet that busted the back window was stuck in the dashboard directly in front of my face. If I would not have ducked when I did, that bullet would have hit me in the back of the head and killed me. GRACE!

When I looked at Tank on that hospital table, it was also God's grace that allowed me to see that one day, that grace was going to run out. While I was running recklessly through the world, hurting people, destroying lives, and sinning against God, He kept showing me grace; but it wasn't because He was cool with what I was doing. In the Bible, in the book of Romans, chapter 2, verses 4 and 5; it says this: "Don't you see how wonderfully kind, tolerant, and patient God is with you? Does this mean nothing to you? Can't you see that his kindness is intended to turn you from your sin?"

God shows us grace while we are doing the worst things in the world, not so we can keep on doing them, but so we see that love, turn from our sin, and turn to Him to ask for forgiveness. But instead, we use God's grace like our own personal ATM, and we make withdrawals whenever we need it most. Whether it's in the back of a police car, in an abandoned building with a needle stuck in our arm about to overdose, in a holding cell waiting to be booked, in a hospital recovering from a bullet wound, embezzling millions of dollars, waiting on an AIDS test, a pregnancy test, wherever we find ourselves needing grace, we make a withdrawal; and as soon as we are in the clear, we go back to normal.

I couldn't go back to normal after what I had experienced in that jail cell. This time it was obvious to me that I had experienced God's grace, and my response was to turn to God. God didn't show me grace just to free me from that jail cell. God didn't show me grace just so I could have a cool story to tell. He showed me grace so I could repent, so He could free me from my sin and save my soul. I remember my granny once told me, "Go to God and talk to Him in whatever way you talk. He will understand." When I prayed to God in that cell, it was probably the most hood prayer He had ever heard...but He heard it.

I could not have made up a better story that paints a picture of our walk through this world and the gospel: I was born on a plantation, a place where people were once physically slaves, and even though I wasn't a slave physically, spiritually I was born one. The day I walked out of that jail cell, I was reborn, and I was set free. All of my life I believed that because of where I lived, the color of my skin, my daddy being gone, my mother doing what she was doing, I felt like I was made to be what I saw around me every day. I thought all that I could ever be was a drug dealer, a killer, robber, etc., but that's a lie.

Here are a couple things the Bible says about us being created and why:

God created us.
All things were made through him, and without him was not any thing made that was made. –John 1:3
No matter what the circumstances when you were conceived and came to this world, you are not a mistake. God created you. A lot of us walk through this world feeling like we are a mistake, asking why were we created and feeling like we don't have a reason to live. God does not make mistakes. You were created on purpose, with a purpose, and don't let anyone tell you differently. The best way to find out about why you were created is to read the owner's manual, the Bible.

You were created in God's image.

So God created man in his own image, in the image of God he created him; male and female he created them. *–Genesis 1:27*

Not only are you not a mistake, you are not worthless. This world has a way of making us feel worthless because of the things we don't have, the things others do have, how we look, how others treat us, or how we see ourselves. We determine our worth and beauty from the opinions or appearance of others, who are just as fragile as we are. The same God that created the universe created you. Out of all the things that exist in the world, He made us after His image.

God created you to do good works.

For we are his workmanship, created in Christ Jesus for good works, which God prepared beforehand, that we should walk in them. –Ephesians 2:10

I know what it's like to feel like a failure. When you feel like nothing you do is right or feeling like you've done so much wrong that you are just the worst person in the world. When we walk and live in the darkness this world has to offer, our best deeds are trash in God's sight. When we turn from our sin and turn to our Creator we not only experience grace, but we also walk into the good works that we were created to do. You were created by God to bring something good to this world, to be a light in darkness. It doesn't matter if you have landed in jail on a life sentence, there is still room for you to repent and walk into good works.

I just knew, like everybody around me, that I would be dead or in jail before I was eighteen. Go to any ghetto, hood, inner city, whatever you want to call it, and find the young boy or girl who has no father around, a mom with drug issues, and you have me. Your story may be different from ours; your identity issues may have come through having too much. Even if that is your story, all of our issues are rooted in the same thing—sin. Every human being on this earth, from the richest to the poorest, the shortest to the tallest, all have one thing in common that links us together. We are all sinners. We were born into a sinful world. There is no amount of money, good deeds, or social status that can pay sin's debt. The only payment acceptable for sin is the sacrifice made on the cross by the Savior, Jesus the Christ. The good news is, we don't have to work for it. That's why it's called grace; all we have to do is ask forgiveness.

For by grace you have been saved through faith. And this is not your own doing; it is the gift of God, – Ephesians 2:8

We survive in situations that seem hopeless, trials on top of trials, and it seems like it's going to destroy us. If you take a closer look, you may see God's grace, shaping a beautiful story of redemption. I am human and I would be lying if I said I didn't have some regrets about my life, some things that I wish I could change. A lot of days I thought I was going to lose, but I fought and won, against all the odds. By the grace of God, when I walked out of that jail cell, I was given another chance at life. I was given another chance to be who God created me to be. What about you, are you going to be who God created you to be?

SPECIAL DEDICATION

This book is dedicated to the memory of Richard Spurlock, Sr., the only daddy I ever had and wanted. We reconciled our differences and began building a better relationship over the years. He helped start my music career and gave me pointers that changed the way I do shows. I wanted so much more from him, because I love him, but I am grateful for the time we had. My greatest honor in this world was to carry you to the place where your body would lie. I wish I had you 100 more years, and I miss you so much. The day I heard you say you were proud of me took away all of the pain. I love you, Pops. There will never be a man that can fill this place in my heart that you have. I'm still fighting to make you proud.

FORGIVE ME

I want to ask forgiveness of every woman, mother, father, and family, of anyone that I've ever hurt walking through this life. I was young, misguided, and acting fully in the sin nature that we are all born with. It goes without saying that there are a lot of things that I wish I could take back and do over, but I can't. Even though God has forgiven me, there is a thorn in my side that I carry with me. It constantly reminds me of the pain I've caused others, but also of the grace that I have received.

I, too, have lost a lot in life and have lost a lot of people that I loved. Wayne, Oscar, Gus, Leo, Lenny, Chris, S.B, Hot Rod, Fred Dog, Y.G., Jerome, Famar (my best friend at that time), Chi, my "big brother" Johnny, Mikey, my little cousin Worm, my cousin Drew, and my best friend and cousin, Tank. There are so many more that I could name. I say all of that to say this: we were all fed a lie. We are taught that we have to destroy our neighbor to survive. I hate that I believed the lie for so many years, and I will fight the rest of my days to rebuild the things that I once helped destroy. I pray that you find peace, hope, forgiveness, and new life in the same place where I found it—our Creator, Jesus.

Travis Thi'sl Tyler

AGAINST ALL ODDS

Against All Odds may be purchased in bulk
for educational, business, fundraising,
or sales promotional use.

For information, please email
BulkOrders@AllOddsBook.com

Twitter | Instagram | Facebook | YouTube

@ThisI

Music | Merch | Tour Dates

www.IamThisl.com